Wakefield Press

Temples and Tuk Tuks

Born into the farming community of Caltowie in the mid north of South Australia, Lydia Laube gained her nursing qualifications at the Royal Adelaide and Calvary Hospitals in Adelaide and then set off to see the world. She worked in Darwin, Papua New Guinea, Hong Kong, London, Italy, Indonesia and, finally, Saudi Arabia, the experience which led her to write her first best-seller, *Behind the Veil*. Her story of her travels in Cambodia, *Temples and Tuk Tuks*, is her sixth book.

T0359715

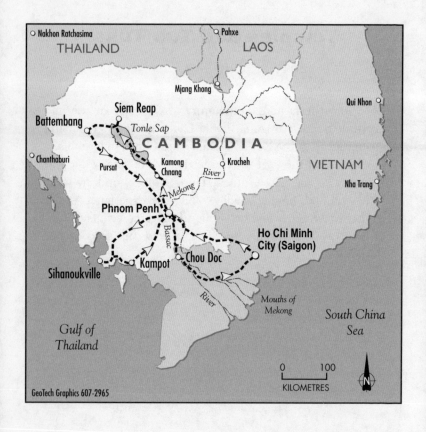

Temples
and Tuk Tuks

Travels in Cambodia

LYDIA LAUBE

**Wakefield
Press**

Wakefield Press
1 The Parade West
Kent Town
South Australia 5067
www.wakefieldpress.com.au

First published 2003
Reprinted 2009

Cover designed by Lahn Stafford Design
Typeset by Clinton Ellicott, Wakefield Press, Adelaide
Printed and bound by Hyde Park Press, Adelaide

National Library of Australia
Cataloguing-in-publication entry

Laube, Lydia, 1948–   .
Temples and tuk tuks: travels in Cambodia.

ISBN-13: 978 1 86254 631 8.
ISBN-10: 1 86254 631 2.

1. Laube, Lydia, 1948–   – Travel. 2. Cambodia – Description
and travel. 3. Vietnam – Description and travel. I. Title.

915.04

Contents

1 At Last – Cambodia   1

2 Choeung Ek – The Killing Fields   22

3 Tuol Seng, Security
  Prison Number 21   44

4 Temples and Tuk Tuks   53

5 Angkors Aweigh to
  the Bamboo Train   74

6 Doctor Evil and the Wild West   99

7 Encounters of the Spooky Kind   120

8 Lady of the Lake   152

9 Chou Doc – No Pain, No Gain   173

1 At Last – Cambodia

Singapore Airlines unsportingly took my knitting needles from me at Adelaide airport. Perhaps they thought that I might stick up the pilot and purl and plain him into submission.

How was I now supposed to tranquillise my white knuckles? Knitting is my antidote to fear of flying. I can't read, especially at take off or landing, in case I miss something sinister.

I survived the take-off sans knitting, and even the food was good – and came early because I'd ordered a diabetic meal (I'm not a diabetic, but saying so gets you better food). The flight was as smooth as silk and the skies were clear all the way.

At half past five in the evening I arrived in Singapore. I was on my way to Vietnam, destination Cambodia. I had waited a long time for this. The barbaric Khmer Rouge regime and the bloody civil war that followed it had turned Cambodia into a tragic place of horror and danger that prevented travellers going there for over twenty years. Finally, relative tranquillity has returned and although land mines, bandits and the odd guerrilla still exist, parts of Cambodia are no longer restricted and are reasonably safe. Small numbers of visitors are now venturing into the country. Now at last I could make the journey I'd had to cancel when I had been in Vietnam and so close to Cambodia five years before.

The next flight out to Ho Chi Minh City was not until half past nine the next morning, so the airline was obliged to provide me with a cost-free stopover at a city hotel. Waiting ages for my bag to appear joy-riding on the rondel, I presumed

1

that this was 'the last bag off syndrome', which is routine for me. But this time it was 'no bag off'! The horrible idea finally dawned on me that my luggage may have been booked through all the way to Vietnam.

Sure enough it had. The staff in lost property said that the plane was still on the tarmac, but it would take an hour to retrieve my bag. I waited. No bag appeared. After ninety minutes they sent me off to one of the airport's many restaurants with a twenty-five dollar voucher for dinner. What a great barn of a place Changi Airport is. It took me half an hour to find the restaurant, directed hither and thither and finally taken to it by a kind soul. By the time I did locate it, I was thoroughly cheesed off. The food was not very good, but it made me feel better.

I gave up on the bag at nine o'clock and took the airport bus to my hotel. Riding through the warm tropical night I saw that Singapore still looked much the same as the last time I had been here: the lush green parks and gardens, stacks of high-rise buildings, blaze of downtown neon and stupendous hotels that looked impossibly high. And everything was squeaky clean.

I was given a suite on the fourteenth floor (what if a fire broke out!) that was super swish. I'd almost had a fit when I had seen the list of prices at the desk. My room cost six hundred and fifty Singapore dollars – that's even more in Australian dollars. I consider it utterly decadent to spend so much on a night's rest. I could pay for the total care of two Cambodian orphans for a year for that.

I didn't have much time to enjoy the kitchen, dining room and king-size bed and I pondered the usefulness of putting my ten-dollar fake pearls in the safe. Lying in the bathtub, restoring my equilibrium, I cast a critical eye over the grouting of the tiles and decided that it was a worse job than I could have done. I'm a grouting connoisseur since I did all the tiles in my own bathroom. I was almost asleep when my bag finally caught up with me around midnight.

An automatic wake-up call from a machine forced me out of bed at six and I fell onto the bus to return to the airport at half past. I was surly about this as the plane for Vietnam didn't leave for three hours and, what was worse, I had not touched the money I had exchanged on arrival to use in Singapore. Fat lot of use that was going to be now.

It was a very bumpy flight through a cloudy sky to Ho Chi Minh City, but the sight of the female airport staff floating gracefully about in their sky-blue and white ao dais lifted my spirits. The airport, however, was a far cry from my previous entry to Vietnam, when I had walked alone over a bridge across the beautiful river that forms the border with China in the north. Here it was a nightmare. You stand in an un-airconditioned hall in incredibly long rows for an interminable time. The rows are long and slow moving due to the communist fervour, or suspicion, that makes the officials take forever to process each person. It was more than an hour before I reached the immigration desk. Then it was on to the customs line.

After two hours I tottered outside and the steamy tropical heat hit me, a sensation about as pleasant as a slap in the face with a wet fish. Considering that the temperature had been five degrees when I had left Australia only a short while before, it was quite a shock. Hijacked by a waiting taxi driver, I allowed him to take me to the small family-run Hotel Van Tran in the traveller's part of town that he recommended.

This hotel was a narrow, high-rise building that possessed no lift. Naturally I was billeted as near to the sky as possible at the top of cardiac-arrest inducing stairs. I arrived panting and fell on the bed to sleep until dinner time.

My room had a dinky balcony that I could only reach by stepping halfway behind the wardrobe. Not a metre wide, the balcony was just big enough to harbour a fold-up chair and a weeny bit of wrought iron that someone had thoughtfully put across the front to stop you pitching nose first into the street – but it gave me a great eagle-eye view of the small, busy street below. The room was neat, but freezing, and the airconditioner had been hot-wired with duct tape to a power cord up near the ceiling.

In the evening I walked around the corner to eat at Kim Café, a well-known traveller's hangout, and ordered what had been a favourite of mine when I had eaten there before, chicken pho. Nothing had changed, not even the prices or the staff. I sat at the front where the café is open to the constant activity of the street where women swung by with baskets loaded with vegetables and fruit on their shoulder poles, or stopped to set up tiny food stalls on the footpath. It was good to be back being offered morning glory greens and soursops and having my coffee served in a dripper pot perched over a glass mug. I asked for fruit salad and was presented with enough for four hungry people – a wheelbarrow load of colourful goodies arranged in a pleasing pattern on a large plate. Perusal of the menu informed me that you could still get absolutely blotto for a couple of dollars. That is if you were not too fussy about the source of the hard 'likker'. Fruit juice was fifty cents, adding 'rum' cost just twenty cents more.

I got lost going home. The street was dark and poorly lit and I was walking up it for the third time when I spied the hotel manager waving at me from across the road. I had no trouble falling asleep again despite the constant noise from the street below and when I woke in the middle of the night everything was quiet except for the sound of heavy rain. In the morning I surfaced slowly to Sally Forth (I always wonder just who she is) with a cyclo recruited for me by the manager. By the time I reached the Ben Thanh market, a huge, fascinating, but rather airless place, it had started to rain again, so I bought a pink brolly to replace the decrepit one I was carrying. As I left the market a Buddhist nun in grey robes proffered her begging bowl and smiled sweetly at me.

In the street I found that it was still raining. I hailed a

cyclo, whose rider installed me and then proceeded to wrap me in plastic like a mummy, leaving only a wee bit of my face out to delight the passing motorists. I suppose he figured that it didn't matter if that got wet.

Cyclos are a most civilised way to get about. When I had been negotiating the fare with the rider he had said, 'Ten,' and I held up what I thought were ten fingers in agreement. He said, 'Okay, okay,' and on arrival I gave him ten thousand dong and he gave me one thousand back. Then I realised that he had counted my fingers. I only have nine.

The rain was lovely. I stood on my dinky balcony to watch it cleaning and cooling the streets. Now, as I noticed the water falling off their edges, I realised that the straw coolie hats many women wear act as mini umbrellas. A man in grubby orange overalls pushed a dilapidated rubbish collection cart up the street. The cart was piled with the small plastic bags of garbage that people heave out into the gutters in the hope that someone will remove them. Around the corner zoomed a large dog on a motorbike. I looked again. No, it was a dog sitting on a girl's lap, its paws up on the handlebars as though it was driving.

Later I rode pillion on a motorbike, the alternative transport to cyclos, to the post office. I was having trouble adjusting to the heat and the French-built post office, lovely as ever, was still a good place for a bit of respite. When I changed some money I was surprised to find that an Australian dollar was worth 8500 dong, half as much again as it had been five years ago, but despite this prices didn't seem to have increased very much. You could still get a good deal at a small hotel for ten to twenty Australian dollars.

After siesta I patronised a café that had just that day opened for business. I was their first, and so far their only, customer and the staff fell over themselves to be nice to me. They sat me on the street front, confident no doubt that my presence would entice others in. I hoped that I looked a good advertisement for food. I couldn't say the same for the menu, which offered, among other delicacies, humbugger and dried friend. After an excellent meal of fried rice and vegetables they presented me with a free fruit salad.

Across the street I saw a sign that advertised 'Foot Massage' and decided to have one. Sitting in the entrance hall of this frowsy, rather strange establishment, I faced the usual Buddhist shrine and altar that hung on the wall. Then I did a double take. Above the joss sticks and offerings loomed Sitting Bull, hatchet face, war paint and full feather headdress.

A girl appeared, took me by the hand and, lifting a key off a board by the stairs, led me to a dingy corridor where she unlocked a door and ushered me into a grotty room that contained only a double bed. I saw people coming and going through other doors before she shut and locked the door after us. The girl gave me a cake of soap and pointed to an adjoining dank hole of a bathroom. I presumed that she wanted me to wash my feet. (Perfectly understandable – nobody would want to get near my unwashed tootsies.) She went outside for a while and on her return seemed surprised that I still had on all my clothes. Pointing down, I said, 'Only feet.'

I began to wonder if 'foot massage' might have been a euphemism for something else. Or maybe the sign was Full Massage mis-spelt. My masseur had no English and my Vietnamese is nil, so I submitted to my fate. She put me on the bed, rolled my trousers up to the knee, jumped onto the bed with me and, kneeling between my legs, started beating hell out of them. With her hands joined together in an attitude of prayer, she rabbit-chopped me all the way from my thighs down to my ankles. When she made it to my feet she did the same to them. It felt like bastinado, the torture where they beat your feet with a cane. Next she took handfuls of the flesh of my legs and pinched her way from my feet to past my knees, up one side and down the other, creeping ever further up my thighs. When this girl gets to my groin, I thought, I am going to tell her that my foot ends there.

Next she started punching my thighs with fists that were like mini sledgehammers. By now I was certain that this little madam had it in for me. But I kept quiet lest she become even more violent, consoling myself with the thought that it couldn't last for too long. It went on and on for an hour and ten minutes exactly.

At one stage she pulled me up and indicated that she wanted to get at my neck, but I drew the line at that. 'No way, lady!' I said, 'You are not rampaging around my neck.' I could end up a quadriplegic. So she took hold of my toes and started twisting them as though she had a pair of old sandshoes in her hands. I imagined I heard the sound of bones breaking.

Released from my tormenter at last, I emerged to freedom feeling surprisingly good in the feet department, as if I was limping on air.

Later, riding around downtown Saigon, I realised that I had forgotten what it was like to be hurled at traffic head-on in a cyclo, or scooted around on the back of a motorbike. There were even more of the latter now; everyone and everything was on one of these mechanical atrocities. Once my cyclo pulled up beside a motorbike that had a mother and three ten-year-old girls scrunched onto it. A beaming girl held up a plastic jar that contained an enormous black cricket. Almost all women out riding wore long, coloured gloves up to their armpits and scarves to filter the traffic fumes tied across their faces that transformed them into slim, dainty bandits. Western dress is now common, but you still see girls all pretty and elegant in their ao dais.

I had bought a bus ticket to Cambodia from an office in the street next to the hotel. The bus left at the respectable hour of nine and cost the princely sum of eleven dollars – or a satisfactory dollar ten per hour for the ten-hour trip.

One of the hotel family escorted me to the bus, trundling

my bag after him. I climbed aboard behind a couple of young, saffron-robed Buddhist monks, taking care not to contaminate them with my touch – women are not supposed to touch monks – and found a seat among the other passengers, who were all Cambodian or Vietnamese – I couldn't tell the difference yet. The driver told me that it was 'two and a half hours on the good road to the border and a long time after that on the bad road'.

As we inched our way, bumping, lurching and jolting through the crowded streets, I decided that if this was the good road, I wasn't anxious to meet the bad one. It took an eon to clear the town and we were still not out of the built-up area. It was much later before I saw a piece of green here and there, or a bullock or ox standing around in between the areas of dense housing.

Halfway to the border the bus stopped for refreshments. The toilet here was a tiled floor with a hole in it and this was where I discovered that the small tear in the cartilage of my left knee that I had recently acquired was not about to accommodate a squat toilet. Getting down was a breeze but I almost didn't make it up again.

At Moc Bai, the Cambodian–Vietnamese border crossing, we were herded off the bus and someone grabbed my bag, a porter I hoped. No man's land lay before me, a long, shadeless stretch of rough, broken dirt, useless for a suitcase on wheels. I chased after my bag and was led to immigration, an abysmal dump housed in a narrow, airless adobe hut where crowds of people from several buses stood for hours in what, thanks to the efforts of a couple of very large, bronzed Anzacs of the New Zealand variety, eventually became a queue.

Just one official manned the hole of an office in a corner of the hut and he had the mammoth task of processing all these people. The local folk obviously did not approve of queuing and some simply refused to go to the end of the line, which by now stretched to the far end of the building. The man behind me was a tour guide who clutched a stack of passports. The two Buddhist monks strolled up and inserted themselves in the line. This was obviously quite acceptable. No one complained. One older woman would not stop trying to shove in and was repulsed again and again until a Cambodian man took her passport and passed it in with his. Other people slithered up to the office side door, shoved their passports onto the desk and had them stamped and returned. I suspected that the passports contained money.

After more than an hour I was at last free to look for my bag. I hadn't been able to see it for the crowd and I'd simply had to trust the man who was looking after it. I spotted it lying flat against a wall, moonlighting as a picnic table for a lady who squatted on her haunches beside it with her two tiny toddlers. My porter picked up the bag, dusted off the rice and other remnants of their feast, hoisted it onto his shoulder and we set off again on another long hike over more broken ground and rubble to the custom department's hut. I presented my passport, was allowed to pass and, walking through a gate decorated with twining dragons under the red and blue national flag, I arrived in Cambodia.

Cambodia is in the heart of Indochina. Covering 181,035 square kilometres, it is little more than half the size of Vietnam, but has borders with Thailand, Laos and Vietnam. Despite this, the country has managed to remain uniquely Khmer. Cambodian culture, which is older than Thailand's, was influenced by Indian, not Chinese or Vietnamese ways. Although it is one of the poorest countries on earth, where it is not scarred by its terrible recent past it is a land of extreme beauty, whose people, despite their poverty, are friendly and cheerful. The climate, however, is another matter. You can choose between hot, or hot and wet.

The Cambodian immigration hut was just big enough to accommodate two officers, one male and one female, inside its hallowed halls, so the line formed outside. Thank goodness it was nowhere near as long as the last one had been, but as I moved slowly along in the sun filling out the required form – I've become pretty good at filling out forms on the run – I felt sweat running down my back and dripping off in rivulets. The man stamping the passports was getting through them rapidly. The woman assisting him smiled at me and intimated that I should lift my sunglasses. I did and she said she liked my earrings. I think.

Another long hike ensued, this time with another porter. On reaching the Cambodian side my previous porter, after some serious negotiations, had sold me to this one while I stood by like a slave on the auction block.

From here I was to travel in a mini bus that belonged to the Capital guesthouse in Phnom Penh.

The bus waited beside a thatched roof over a piece of cement that, for want of a better word, I shall call a restaurant. We weren't due to leave for an hour, so I pointed to some bits of ancient chicken and unidentifiable green stuff that sat forlornly on a shelf awaiting an owner, and smothered my plate with chilli as a prophylactic. Fortunately, the Cambodian coffee turned out to be even better than Vietnamese, black, strong and full of flavour. It was served in a medicine-sized glass that sat in a bowl of hot water. Why they felt the need to keep it warm in the great heat was a puzzle.

I paid the tiny sum asked of me and requested directions to the loo. A woman waved me out the back, where I spied numerous tiny huts, and investigated the washhouse and the chicken coop, until someone directed me to an edifice innocent of a roof and entirely, including the door, made of woven rattan pieces. There was no latch. You just pushed the rattan aside and once inside shoved it to. A very nice banana tree kept me company.

Back on the bus I decided that the country didn't appear very different from Vietnam, except that the occasional house I saw was poorer looking. After a while small villages began to appear beside the road. In 1998 the first census in decades found that there were around eleven and a half million Cambodians, eighty-five percent of whom live in the country and survive on agriculture. Another seventy thousand hill tribesmen and women live in the mountains. Life expectancy is only fifty-one years, one child in five dies before the age of five due to poverty and disease and half the population is under fifteen.

The country already looked wet and then it started to rain again. The road was absolutely ghastly, worse even than the road I had classed as the worst in the world – Bolivia's only road through its north. This road was one car wide and some of it had once been bitumen, but was now full of potholes the size of bomb craters. I discovered that the only way to survive was to ride the bus like a horse. Grabbing the seat in front of me, I planted my feet on the floor and lifted saddle with the worst of the bumps. It was utterly teeth jarring; you wouldn't have dared try to eat anything. I attempted drinking from my bottle, but the water flew out of it at one huge jolt and landed on the poor man sitting in front of me. The second time I ended up with water in my mouth, but the bottle almost down my throat. I tried to scratch my nose and nearly poked out my eyeball. Reinserting a hairpin that had shaken loose, I all but punctured my eardrum.

The bus stopped for a break after two hours, but by then I wanted merely to sit still for a minute. The road was now just dirt dotted here and there with roadworks and machinery, which, as far as I could see, had caused no improvement. In front of the houses were shallow dams in which buffalo, and occasionally people, wallowed up to their necks in muddy water. Fields of rice and sugarcane were interspersed among wooden-framed dwellings with sides of woven palm mats or wooden planks and thatched or tin roofs. Most of them stood on wooden stilts.

Every abode had its spirit house perched on a stand in

front of it and a large stoneware jar to catch water off the roof. Spirit houses are made of the same materials as the house they protect. You could hardly put the spirit who owns the place into a lesser house than you have, so the ones outside houses of sticks and thatch were made of sticks and thatch and later, when there was the odd brick house with a tiled roof, its spirit house would be made of brick or stone with a little tiled roof that had brightly painted, curly edges.

Now and then we passed through a village where a fancy pagoda, gilded and painted yellow and red, stuck out from the drab houses like a sore thumb. Further towards the capital I began to see the odd stupendous fence and gate made of beautiful, multi-coloured, decorative ironwork behind which, looking incongruous, would be crouched a stick and iron humpy, or a modest stone dwelling.

Children waved to the bus as we went by and once we stopped to allow a boy, riding one buffalo and towing another, to cross the road. We passed bullock carts loaded with hay or sugarcane, white Brahmin-type cows tethered by the roadside and a truck that was packed full of pigs and had a line of men sitting on top of its side rails wearing kramas, the traditional black and white scarves, wrapped around their heads. There was a fair amount of traffic, but at least this road was flat – although at times we did skid from one shoulder of the road to the other, tipping alarmingly and threatening to go over the edge into the ditch. But ditches don't scare me. And hadn't I vowed never to complain about any road again after the horrors of the Andes? At least here I wasn't skittering along in mud on the edge of a mountain precipice.

The road crossed a couple of bridges spanning big rivers and eventually the houses started to look grander. After five hours, by when I thought the road would never end, we drove onto a ferry and crossed the Mekong River. A little later, after fording the bridge over the Bassac River, we were in the outskirts of Phnom Penh.

My first impressions of Cambodia's capital city were not good. This looked a dismal sort of place, with skinny, multi-storeyed houses crammed together in constricted streets that were crowded with motorbikes, bicycles and cyclos.

By the time I was released from the grip of the bus I was a wreck. Standing on the pavement, still shaking from the vibrations, I felt pulverised all over. There was no way I was going any further so I told the Capital staff, who had come out to waylay travellers, that I gladly accepted their kind offer of a roof over my head.

The Capital has a pretty good lurk. They send a bus down to meet the people off the Vietnamese bus, and its terminus in Phnom Penh is their guesthouse. You are more or less a captive customer – by the time you have suffered hours of the horrible Cambodian road all you want to do is fall in the nearest bed. You arrive shaken, bruised and battered, it's getting dark, and the streetlights are coming on. Where else would you go?

There are three Capital guesthouses, eloquently named Numbers One, Two and Three. I chose the latter, as it was the newest, and procured a lad to carry my bag. The entrance is down a tiny, dusty alley with a broken footpath, where you have to fight your way through a thousand parked bicycles. A narrow, uninspiring entrance between two unattractive buildings breaks out into a foyer about two metres wide. Here a smiling young man and woman waited behind a minuscule counter to greet me with the traditional sompiah. Like a Thai wai, they pressed their hands together in prayer and bowed. Everyone in Cambodia seemed so young – maybe because the Khmer Rouge killed off so many people and the ones who were left haven't had a chance to get old yet. The pleasant young couple said that they didn't have a single room, but would let me have a double at the same price providing I promised not to use the air-conditioning. A fan was fine with me and the room was perfectly adequate, except that no amount of banging knobs and twisting buttons would make the hot water system live up to its name.

As soon as I had washed and powdered my nose, I went down to Capital Number One's café. Standing on a semi-circular corner that was mostly open to the surrounding traffic noise, pollution and heat, the café was completely encircled by stationary motorbikes waiting for trade, while multitudes more swirled past. A platoon of blue plastic chairs surrounded a few metal tables and a tatty tin awning that formed a veranda shade by day was pulled down to lock up the café at night. I found a seat under a fan and ate a breast of a chicken submerged in a big dish of green, sloppy stuff. It tasted delicious and contained a surprising amount of meat for a meal in an Asian country. I tried the local Angkor beer, brewed by an Australian joint venture in Sihanoukville on the south coast. It was okay, but not as good as West End and expensive compared to the food, which was exceedingly cheap. There were plenty of fruit juices and Chinese-type tea is always provided free of charge.

In one corner of the café there was a counter for changing money and booking tours. I bought twenty US dollars worth of riel and, at four thousand to the dollar, received an enormous wad of notes. When I asked the helpful man about the tours, he said, 'Don't go out in the afternoon, it's too hot.' He also told me that it was safe to go down by the river in the evening, but not to walk anywhere after dark.

Before the end of the civil war in the late 1990s, Cambodia had been a very difficult and dangerous place in which to travel, especially since the Khmer Rouge began targeting foreigners in that decade. Kidnap and murder were real possibilities for those brave enough to risk travelling in Cambodia then. It had put me off. Five years before I had sat in Saigon trying to summon the nerve to take the ferry to the southern Cambodian port of Sihanoukville and the train from there to Phnom Penh. I chickened out when three tourists were kidnapped off that train and subsequently murdered. Even now I was warned not to be lulled into a false sense of security. Cambodia is still a lawless country and hazards persist. The political situation remains unstable and you need to check the state of security as you go. Because of bandits and guerrillas the roads in some areas are not safe. There are plenty of guns around and they are said to be often used, while land mines also continue to kill and injure many people. However, as far as I could deduce, terrorists of the bombing variety did not exist.

Phnom Penh is reputed to be the most dangerous place of all. I read that robberies are frequent here, and that if you are accosted, you should let bandits have your goodies without making a fuss.

Calling an end to my first day in Cambodia I fell on my bed and was soon asleep. But not for long. The room had a big window that opened onto the wall of the next building, only a few centimetres away, where many local people lived with an overabundance of children. Even through my earplugs I could hear screaming kids and loud conversations that went on for hours.

What with the combined efforts of the bus and the masseur who had inflicted grievous bodily harm on me, I woke up late and creaking and was not ready to face the world until the aspirin I swallowed kicked in. At breakfast in the corner café I ordered eggs, but made the mistake of saying toast because I didn't know how to say bread. Instead of a yummy baguette I was given two hunks of square, yellow-tinted stuff that tasted like bad cake. There was no butter. I ladled the eggs onto one of the pieces of alleged bread and consumed the other one dry. While I ate, boys wanting work as my moto driver, or shoe shiner, pestered me and a woman sold me a newspaper for seventy-five cents. I discovered later that if you don't want to buy a paper, you could hire it for the duration of breakfast.

The weather was extremely hot and humid and I didn't feel

like walking around, so I returned to my room and holed up until after siesta. Even at breakfast I'd had sweat pouring from me which, for someone who normally can't get a glow up, was a surprise. The boy from the guesthouse hailed a cyclo for me and established the price I should pay to be taken to the river. There were no taxis for private hire. A cyclo, a three-wheeled bicycle with a seat in front for a passenger, or a moto – the pillion of a motorbike – are the ways to get about.

The corniche that runs beside the river is the upmarket part of Phnom Penh, which, sited at the confluence of the Bassac, Tonle Sap and Mekong rivers, was once said to be the loveliest of the French-built cities of Indochina. Legend says that the city was created because an old woman called Penh found four Buddha images washed up on the bank of the Mekong. She placed them on a nearby hill, Phnom Penh, the Hill of Penh, and a town grew up around it. Wat Phnom, the city's main temple, is located on top of a twenty-seven-metre, tree-covered knoll, the only elevation in town. In the 1440s, Phnom Penh replaced the previous capital, Angkor, because it was better located for river trade with Laos, China and Indonesia. By the mid sixteenth century Phnom Penh had become a regional power.

Walking along the promenade, where some of Phnom Penh's former charm can still be seen, I came to the Renakse Hotel, an old colonial institution. I thought it would be great to stay in this hotel and absorb some atmosphere of the past, so, after a courteous young man let me inspect a room, I booked it for the next day. The room was comparatively expensive – nearly fifty dollars (Australian – I only think in Aussie dollars) but it was quaint and comfortable.

The Renakse is opposite the royal palace, so it is certainly in the right part of town. As I ambled past the front of the palace, through the iron gates I noticed a bloke wearing only a sarong having a wash under a hose on the lawn. He was possibly the gardener. I don't think the king takes his ablutions in public.

The National Museum is a little north of the palace and as I neared it rain began to pelt down in a real tropical storm. A couple of French people thundered past me, sploshing and splashing. Not long before they had been sniggering at my parasol – now I smirked at them. At the museum gate I was hit a hefty admission fee and realised too late that I had committed the awful boo boo of taking my change with my left hand.

The museum building is spectacular. Built in 1917 of dark red, purplish terra-cotta bricks in a beautiful traditional Khmer design, it looks as though it was made yesterday. Its multiple-tiered, tiled roofs lift at each corner like those of pagodas and it has lovely gardens that surround four sizeable ponds containing water lilies, lotus flowers and golden carp. I hadn't imagined that Phnom Penh would have stunning buildings like this, or that they and the royal palace would still be standing after all the unrest the country has endured.

Inside the museum a teacher led a group of children about. She was rabbiting on beside a showcase of pottery, but the kids were engrossed in the goldfish in the pool beside it. There were some beautiful bronzes, battalions of wonderful stone Buddha statues and many porcelain pieces, some of which were labelled 'Provenance Unknown' but looked like Thai Sawankhalok to me.

I stopped to rest for a while in the quiet and shaded grounds before passing through the large park, with what looked like a football oval in its middle, that stands in front of the museum. Many people, surrounded by much litter, were camped around the fringes of the park. I later learnt that they were peasants from drought-stricken provinces. They had come to seek help from the king, who traditionally gives food to his people in times of trouble.

On the riverfront I entered a small shop that advertised overseas phone calls and tried to do an ET and 'call home'. It didn't cost much as, due to the six-second delay, all I managed to scream was 'hello', and 'goodbye'. I decided that it would be better to wait until I knew that everyone would be in bed and leave a message on a mobile. That way I could say what I needed to without interruptions.

I sat down at a café, which was a big mistake. As soon as I took a chair, a child came along begging. I gave her a small riel note and this opened the floodgates. Hordes of people who wanted something mobbed me. If I had given in to all the shoeshine boys who approached me – poor little kids – I would have had the cleanest shoes in Phnom Penh, if not the world. Forty per cent of Cambodia's population is poor. Half the government's annual budget comes from foreign aid. There is no social security but, fortunately for the needy, it is Buddhist tradition to give alms to the poor.

A moto rider who spoke English helped me negotiate a ride back to the Capital in a cyclo. Being pushed head-on at the traffic was the same terrifying experience as in Vietnam. The trick is not to look if you want to preserve some vestiges of sanity. I don't know how they all miss each other, but they do. It's the same crossing the road. You have to take your courage in your hands and simply walk into the melee and rely on the traffic to avoid you.

One million people now live crammed in the small city of Phnom Penh. In 1970 the population was 500,000. Five years later refugees had swelled it to two million when, on 17 April 1975, two days after Phnom Penh had fallen to them, the Khmer Rouge forced the entire population to march into the countryside. About 1400 Cambodians and foreigners took refuge in the United States Embassy. The Khmer Rouge told the embassy officials that they did not recognise diplomatic privileges and all the Cambodians had to be handed over to them. Most were never seen again. The foreigners were taken out of the country by truck.

Once away from the traffic, being pedalled gently through the back streets in a cyclo is enjoyable. You get to see everything close up and there's only the squeak of the cyclo wheel accompanying you like a demented canary.

I had dinner at the Capital again where the prices are 'traveller' as opposed to the tourist ones I had come across on the corniche. After eating, I went for a short walk to a nearby supermarket. Even at night the main streets are still congested with traffic and I found it disorienting to walk into the dazzling lights of cars when I was not able to see the bikes and cyclos among them. Amazingly, I saw a man walking through the traffic with his back to it.

Phnom Penh's main streets are broken and dilapidated. Minor ones are only rough dirt and they are full of rubbish. This surprised me as the people are very clean and so are the interiors of their houses.

In the supermarket all the prices were in US dollars. There were huge amounts of expensive imported stuff, as well as lots of Asian canned drinks containing exotic fruits and medicinal ingredients such as bird's nests. I invested in some hair spray – what with the fans, open windows, cyclos and motos my hair was standing on end. Now I could nail it to my head with this gunk.

Next morning I paid my huge hotel bill – less than eight dollars – and had an early breakfast in readiness for a tour I had arranged at the Capital café. Now that I had learned how to say bread, I received a hot baguette which, with a scrumptious omelette and coffee, made for an excellent breakfast. I talked to an American gent who had been teaching English in Phnom Penh for six months, but was about to volunteer to work in one of the national parks. He said that he was interested in birds and conservation and that he didn't like living in Phnom Penh. 'It's too crowded, hot, dusty and dirty,' he added. I had to agree with that.

The huge tour bus inched and rumbled along the packed streets. I saw only two traffic lights, which made the way vehicles manage not run into each other even more of an everlasting miracle. In the main road women street-sweepers wearing grass-green lab coats waved spider-web brooms at the gutters. The drab buildings were all squashed together. The houses were narrow and two or three storeys high like those in Vietnam, but not as pretty as many of those are. These were more functional; some were downright dilapidated with rust marks running down from their balconies like tear stains. Clotheslines festooned with washing poked from windows. Misspelt signs gave light relief.

'Department of Management and Economic Antics' – a truer word was never said! 'Foot and Wang Massage' – I wonder how that feels? For that matter where the heck is it? 'Seeing Hands Massage by the Blind' 'Sorear Maternity Clinic' – an apt description.

We passed the Olympic Stadium – I assumed that the name must be a morale booster as they have Buckley's hope of getting the Games there. The stadium is huge with wide flights of steps climbing up to masses of seats. Around its exterior is a tatty, but enormously long, green-painted tin fence, against which a multitude of little businesses operate, mending bikes, selling tubes, doing mechanical repairs, giving hair cuts. Then came a row of fruit stalls brilliant with the countless colours of strange tropical produce that was heaped and piled into artistic designs. I had no idea what many of the fruits were, but I did recognise the hairy bottoms of rambutans.

We crossed a bridge over a river where shanties made of sticks and thatch and the odd bit of tin roosted on spindly sticks in the slush, looking as though they were about to fall down. Close by, in stark contrast to this dreadful sight, a pagoda raised its glittering stupa to the sky, all gold and gorgeous, shining and glinting in the sun.

Although our destination was only fifteen kilometres away from the city, we travelled for an hour to reach it. Turning off the main road, we jolted the last few kilometres along a dirt track that was lined by hovels. Every now and then I spied a reasonable looking house, a bit of rice paddy, some banana trees and the odd cow, but nothing looked organised in the way of cultivation. Beside each house stood the massive stoneware jars that are used as water pots and are seen everywhere. The dirt road's redeeming feature was the gnarled flame trees that lined it and provided a lovely canopy. A small, semi-naked child waved at the bus, his bare bottom hanging out from a shirt that only reached his middle.

Then we came to the killing fields.

2 Choeung Ek –
The Killing Fields

I had imagined that the killing fields would be a vast, dusty paddock, but it is an absolutely beautiful, tranquil place, which makes the abominations committed there seem even worse. At the gate of this former longan orchard, I was confronted by a stupa – a tall, skinny man-made edifice that marks a sacred place – that commemorates the 8985 men, women and children whose remains have been exhumed from mass graves here. Their skulls are piled in the stupa's glass enclosed interior, tier upon tier, up to its tall top. Machete cuts or holes made by sharpened bamboo sticks can clearly be seen on the skulls. The Khmer Rouge saved bullets by bludgeoning or butchering their victims to death.

I asked our guide, a trim young woman, why they had killed the children. She replied, 'Why did they kill anybody?'

I had no idea. I studied the facts, but I never did understand. Except for the nine Westerners who had been included in this carnage, the people the Khmer Rouge killed were not strangers, nor of a different race or creed. They were their own people. That is the most awful fact. It was all so senseless.

The Khmer Rouge – the Red Khmer – regime, was led by Pol Pot, alias Saloth Sar or Brother Number One. On visits to China he had been greatly influenced by the Cultural Revolution, but he did not see its aftermath, or its later failure. When he seized power from Lon Nol, Pol Pot declared 1975 to be Year Zero and set out to eliminate all that had gone before. Money and banks were abolished, books were burned and everyone who was educated was systematically murdered. Village chiefs, schoolteachers and administrators were killed as a matter of course, as well as anyone classed as, or even just thought to be, the intelligentsia.

Pol Pot wanted Cambodia to return to a pure agrarian and peasant society. Two million Cambodians (some say three million) died. The cities were emptied and all urbanites were force-marched into the countryside to work in the fields. Family life was abolished. Deaths resulted from deliberate starvation and overwork: twelve to fifteen hours of hard slave labour per day on hunger rations. Disobedience brought instant execution. It is gruelling just to read this story; what it was like to live it is unimaginable.

Cambodia was cut off from all contact with the outside world, except for a fortnightly flight to Beijing for Chinese aid and advisers. The postal service was abolished. The Khmer Rouge ruled for almost four years. The people can still tell you, 'Three years, eight months and twenty days.' During this time the Khmer Rouge began a border war with the Vietnamese and killed many Vietnamese civilians until, in 1978, Vietnam launched a full-scale invasion of Cambodia in order to over-throw their rule. The defeated Khmer Rouge fled into the jungles and mountains along the Thai border. But even after they were ousted, their evil continued, as they kept Cambodia, which they renamed Kampuchea, in a state of unrest due to the guerrilla war they continued to wage against their country-men. In the chaos the rice crops were either destroyed or not harvested and famine followed. Hundreds of thousands of refugees fled to Thailand.

For most of the 1980s Cambodia was under Vietnamese occupation and closed to the Western world. The United States placed an embargo on the country, the economy was in ruins and more hardship had to be endured. The Khmer Rouge continued guerrilla assaults on the people, terrorising and demoralising them by placing thousands of mines in the roads and rice fields, attacking transport, blowing up bridges and shelling the towns held by the Vietnam-backed government. The town of Pailin, in the north-west near the Thai border, was their stronghold and from there they sold the district's gems and timber that were their source of finance. They also controlled many of the border refugee camps and forced men, women and children to porter supplies and ammunition across land-mined areas.

Thailand supported the Khmer Rouge because they opposed Vietnam. China, Malaysia and Singapore supplied them with weapons, and the British sent the SAS to teach the Khmer Rouge how to use land mines effectively. The US gave large sums of money to the non-communist factions of the Khmer Rouge and they helped the Khmer Rouge coalition retain its seat at the United Nations.

In 1989 Vietnam withdrew all its troops from Cambodia. The Khmer Rouge launched an offensive against the shaky government that was now in control, killing thousands of people and producing 150,000 more refugees. By 1990 diplomatic efforts by the United Nations began to have an effect and non-government organisations were established in Cambodia to provide relief. But the Khmer Rouge remained a legitimate party in the eyes of the United Nations until it was finally disqualified in 1994.

Then the Khmer Rouge began targeting foreign travellers. Six Western tourists were kidnapped and killed in the south, either on the road or the train to Sihanoukville. The plan was to attract the attention of the outside world. It certainly got mine!

The Thais stopped supporting the Khmer Rouge and, severing their border connections, cut off their supply of money. The Cambodian government began a campaign to convince Khmer Rouge fighters to defect. Brother Number Three, Leng Sary, led a mass defection of his three thousand troops from Pailin.

In 1997 Cambodia's coalition government ruptured due to in-fighting and the subsequent coup resulted in more fighting in the streets. Cambodia lost its seat on the United Nations and foreign aid money was cancelled. The next year government forces began an all-out offensive on the rebels in the north and heavy fighting ensued. At this time Pol Pot died and Nuon Cheea, Brother Number Two, defected and made an apology for his barbaric crimes against the people. In the same year Cambodia held its second only election in which the Cambodian People's Party (the CCP) won two-thirds of the votes. This was not enough to govern in its own right, and riots and fighting continued. Now the CCP governs the country in an alliance with FUNCINPEC, the National United Front For An Independent Neutral Peaceful And Co-operative Cambodia as a constitutional monarchy with Hun Sen as the Prime Minister and Norodom Sihanouk as King.

Despite the fact that the Khmer Rouge is ended as a force, several hundred guerrillas still remain at large. Many Cambodian people want the Khmer Rouge tried and punished, but the government is wary of the reaction of the Chinese who supported them and many of whose policies they adopted. Also, for the first time in thirty years Cambodia is at peace and they don't want to stir up the Khmer Rouge again.

I saw Pol Pot interviewed on Australian television not long before his death in 1998 and this monster mass murderer seemed quite benign as he utterly denied any sin.

Walking past the stupa with its grisly contents at the entry gate, I stepped into a pretty green landscape that resembled a golf course. Grassy mounds, interspersed with shady trees, flowering bushes and sweet-scented frangipani, led down to a tree-lined river. It was only after I had moved along the path for a while that I realised, to my distress, that the mounds covered mass graves.

Forty-three of the one hundred and twenty-nine graves are still intact and here and there I saw fragments of cloth and bone protruding from the grass and earth that covered them. From the graves that have been exhumed – pits about four metres square – countless bodies, many bound and blindfolded, have been dug. One pit had a low wooden fence around it, and a roof of palm thatch over it. The bodies of one hundred and thirty women, children and babies had been taken from this site. All the women were naked and almost all had been raped. I stood under a tree next to the pit, and found myself thinking it was pleasantly shady. Then the guide told us that the Khmer Rouge had swung the heads of children against this tree, dashing out their brains. Nearby was a palm tree that had fronds with sharp, serrated edges. These had been used to stab, mutilate, or slice off heads. I felt ill when I saw that it was the same as the palm tree growing in my garden at home.

After this harrowing experience and the added trauma of getting past the flock of tiny child beggars at the gate, we piled back into the bus. No one spoke on the return journey.

I had not intended going to the killing fields, but after a couple of days in Cambodia, I had realised that it is important not to ignore what happened. That would be like rejecting the suffering and saying that the innocent people who died should be forgotten. It is part of Cambodia's history and it is essential to acknowledge it. Cambodians say, 'We must remember, so that it can never happen again. Anywhere.'

Retrieving my bag from the Capital, where I found it sitting at the reception desk guarded by the young lady, I found a moto to transfer me, with the bag up front on the petrol tank, to the Renakse Hotel. On the way we passed a couple of young Buddhist monks in mid-calf saffron robes, who carried colour-coordinated umbrellas, one yellow and one orange. By the time I had checked into my room I was ready for an hour or two on the bed. I couldn't last long outside in this debilitating heat. The temperature reached over 40 degrees at this time of the year, the minimum was only ten degrees less and the heavy carbon monoxide pollution in Phnom Penh wasn't helping me acclimatise.

Later I tottered across the road to visit the royal palace. Inside the grounds I found the palace complex much bigger than it appears from the street, even though it looks pretty stupendous from there. It cost a whacking twelve dollars to get in and a lot more if you wanted your camera to keep you company. I am a lousy photographer, so I didn't bother.

I liked the signs at the entrance. The first one politely stated that they really would rather you didn't bring in firearms and explosives, while another told you to take off your shoes at temples and the throne room, not to wear hats and to dress modestly. I handed my ticket to the guard at the entrance gate. He was taking the cameras of those who hadn't paid for their admission into protective custody and he pointed at my purse, which he thought was a camera, and said, 'Leave here please.'

I said, 'That's my money! You want me to leave my money with you?'

At which all the guards fell about laughing.

The splendours of Cambodian palaces make Versailles look like a slum. The elongated, rectangular throne room of the royal palace is beyond belief. Little tinkling brass bells swing all around the edge of the glittering yellow and green, multi-tiered tiled roof, whose many curved ends reach up for the sky. Inside it is all gold and gleaming decoration and a thousand kilometres long at least. Down its centre rolls an enormous carpet, which must have been especially woven for the room. The carpet ends at the two imposing gold thrones that are flanked by huge, golden Buddha statues. From the centre of the ceiling a succession of massive, dazzling French crystal chandeliers march along the room. The ceiling and the side walls are covered with intricate paintings of scenes from royal life.

Removing my shoes before entering the throne room, I noticed a rack labelled 'Foreigners' Shoes'. Beside it was another rack labelled 'Local People'. Apartheid for shoes? I didn't bother collecting a ticket from the guard for mine. Looking at the line of clunky foreigners' boots that already rested there, I felt safe that no one would swap any of them for my size three flatties.

The palace gardens are immaculate. Most of the plants grow in large ceramic jars or small cement plots and a gardener was moving around watering them with a hefty hose. The king lives in a part of the complex that is off-limits to mere mortals, but the area that is open to the public was still extensive and I took ages to stroll through it. Even under my pink umbrella the day was baking hot, but it was peaceful. The grounds are large enough to amble around and encounter few people, so I felt quite alone with the doves that cooed from the roofs and the birds that sang in the shade trees. Now and then I came upon a part of the garden where I could sit and rest under trees that surrounded me with the scent of their jasmine-like flowers.

The silver pagoda is also in the palace complex. Another very large building, it has a floor entirely made of solid silver tiles and it houses a famous emerald Buddha. Supposedly made of green baccarat glass, not emerald, the Buddha is about half a metre tall and perches high on a pedestal above the other statues that encircle it at eye level. From where I stood it looked as though it could do with a good dusting, but surprisingly it managed to dominate its life-sized, solid-gold neighbours. The foremost gold figure was studded with thousands of old-cut diamonds, some of which were very large and threw out much flashing fire as they caught the light. I wondered how all this loot had managed to avoid Pol Pot. The walls of the silver pagoda are lined with glass museum cases that contain many small Buddhas, as well as hundreds of silver items such as bowls and dishes. Mind you, all the silver could have done with a good clean and polish too.

Another open-sided pavilion contains a life-sized statue of

the king seated on a white horse. And a lovely stupa, dedicated to a long dead princess, reposes on the tip of a steep, skinny knoll that is totally covered in greenery. Around its base, among a profusion of trees, bushes and ferns, nestle miniature grottos that embrace statues of deities.

I climbed up a set of shaded stone steps to the top of the knoll, then moved on to a nearby pavilion that had been donated to the kingdom by Napoleon I. Constructed of grey cast-iron after the manner of the Eiffel Tower, it was home to many more museum pieces in glass cases and a very doddery staircase that bore a warning sign: 'No more than twenty people upstairs, as the floor is not safe'. I waited for a couple of people to come down. I didn't think it was wise to add my fifty-five kilos to the floor without being sure how many people were already up there.

The stupas and pagodas seemed to go on forever, but following the exit signs, I finally came to the way out. The egress led you through a line of souvenir shops that were like running the gauntlet, but I managed to escape without leaving any of my money with them.

I couldn't believe it when I Sallied Forth (that woman again) in the evening and found the air deliciously cool. I think the breeze off the river contributed to this. Hungry, I patronised the nearest source of food, the outdoor restaurant at the side of the Renakse Hotel, where plastic tables and chairs under umbrellas are divided from the wide road outside by trees and shrubs. I ordered chicken curry and rice and a coconut to drink. The curry was like a Thai red curry. The vegetables were good and the juice was smashing, but the chicken was a lucky dip, like finding the shilling in the Christmas pudding. However I *was* presented with a free plate of fruit.

A young man who worked at the restaurant asked if he could sit down and produced a schoolbook with a map of Australia, so that I could show him where I came from. Soon a friend of his also sat down at the table and we talked for about an hour. 'Aren't you busy?' I asked.

He replied that there was hardly anybody in the hotel as they mostly cater for tour groups, especially from France, and there were none at present.

The boys were happy to be able to practise their English on me. They told me that I would be very safe at this hotel, because, as it was near the royal palace, there were always lots of guards close by, as well as police at each end of the street. They don't let just anybody up this road.

That night I was able to sleep without wearing earplugs. The hotel was blissfully quiet once I gave up on the crashing, clanging airconditioner. Sometime during the night I heard the divine drumming of heavy rain on the roof and in the cool early morning I looked out of my window and saw water lying in large puddles in the hotel grounds.

Not that it stayed cool for long. Anticipating this, I decided to get moving as early as possible. Enjoying the slight breeze off the river, I was strolling past the royal palace complex when, as I reached the king's private gates, sixteen police motorbikes roared up with sirens blaring. Three police cars followed them and then they all wheeled about to form a guard lining both sides of the road in front of the gates. I thought, Whacko, the king is coming, and stood waiting under my pink brolly as close as I dared. A Frenchman rushed up with a professional photographer's outfit and set up a tripod. I asked him if he thought the king was coming and he said he presumed so. After a while an excessively large black limousine crept out of the gate and sped away flanked by the police entourage. All I caught sight of was a figure in a suit. No crown, no jewels, nothing. I was monumentally disappointed.

The promenade along the river is very wide and cobble-stone, or tiled, footpaths front the cafés and shops. A road runs beside the footpath and between that and the river is a broad stretch of grass. Not refined enough to call a lawn, it does provide a smidgeon of relief from the concrete. At intervals along the edge of the road, grey-painted, French-colonial iron lampposts stand, separated by red flowering hibiscus bushes. The river's edge is framed by iron balustrades and railings and all along the bank grow a line of spreading trees under which people rest or dangle fishing lines.

I came to the Indochina Hotel, recommended as a good place to buy tickets for boats travelling upriver to Siem Reap, the closest town to Angkor, which was – I hoped – my next destination. Cambodian roads are so bad that when river travel is possible it is best to take it.

In the hotel foyer I found the manager leaning over a mirror picking his pimples. This seemed to be a national pastime; he was the fifth man I had seen engaged in this fascinating hobby. Maybe the climate gives men spots. When the pimple picker desisted from his absorbing occupation, he proved to be the full bottle on information regarding boats. I arranged to buy a ticket on a boat that left in two days time. Mr Tay said that, although it cost a little more, this was the best boat. He also threw in free transport to and from the boat and a discount on a room in Siem Reap, and promised to find out if my Vietnamese visa allowed me to return to Vietnam by boat down the Mekong, entering at Chou Doc, instead of going back to Moc Bai on that ghastly road.

Then I took a cyclo to the central market. I pedalled, or rather the rider did, down a few of the unpaved back streets, sloshing in and out of puddles. Thank goodness there were no hills in Phnom Penh, except for the knoll that Wat Phnom stands on, to make me feel guilty about riding in a cyclo. But if we came to a rise, a puddle or ditch in the road, I would lean forward, like you do to take the weight off the back of a horse when going up a hill, in the hope that this would help the rider. A large sign on a building caught my attention. 'Department for Disasters' – I have encountered a few of those.

And another on a kindergarten: 'The Potential Genius' – it doesn't hurt to hope I guess.

Psar Thmei, Phnom Penh's main market, is a hulking circular edifice that squats smack in the centre of a large space where many roads converge. It badly needed a coat of paint, preferably not of the same bilious mustard hue. Its exterior is encompassed by motorbikes that crowd up to it like bees around a honey pot. Art deco in style, the building's central hall is covered with a high dome made of many panes of glass. Four wings radiate out from the hall and a tall clock, from around which the gold and jewellery stalls fan out, dominates the middle of the central hall. The market's wings contain clothing, pots, pans, electrical goods and more. Name it and it was there. The stalls went on and on. You could get utterly lost and wander around in circles for ages as if you were in a maze.

The building has many entrances, and unfortunately the cyclo rider dumped me at the one to the fish market. It was a case of breath-holding at a gallop until I made it through to the less smelly stuff.

In the central hall I stopped to buy a watch. My old watch had recently died. I bargained a snazzy looking new time-piece down to nine dollars, and then tried to sell Madame my old watch – it only needed a battery, but that was half the price of the new watch. Madame would have none of it. She was no fool and knew rubbish when she saw it – though she was too polite to say so, of course. I had bought that watch in the Andes and it hadn't done too badly to last until Cambodia, considering that it only cost five dollars. Madame altered my new watchband to fit me and I pushed it up under my shirtsleeve in case someone thought it was good enough to pinch.

I decided to buy a gold chain. Eighteen carat gold was ten US dollars per gram in jewellery shops. It was six in the market where there was also leeway for bargaining. No prizes for guessing where I shopped. I found an agreeable little lady in whom I had confidence and later, when I had the gold tested, it was as good as she had said it was. She showed infinite patience with me and we eventually came to an amicable agreement. The sellers sit high above the crowd and the display cases are at eye level. A tiny blue plastic stool was produced for me to stand on and get my chin up to the level of the counter to see the scales. The chain did not have a gold stamp, but the seller said that she would get one for me and led me to the grotty hole in the outer rim of the market where the goldsmiths worked. Under a daggy canvas awning, rows of men, naked to the waist in the intense heat created by dozens of Bunsen burners and blowtorches, sat at rough wooden benches hammering the precious metal.

Wandering further, I bought soap powder and postcards and, desperately in need of fluids, located the food stalls. The menus were chalked on a board in Khmer script. I already knew that the most authentic local food, not to mention prices, is found in places where the prices are in riels, not dollars, but here the prices were not even in Roman numerals and that made it truly local. The food stall eating area was screened from the rest of the market by a row of the ubiquitous blue plastic chairs – they must have got a bulk deal of those from somewhere.

I drank coffee and a bottle of water while watching women cooking and serving various edibles nearby. One woman stood behind a row of big aluminium trays on which were piled the ingredients for making sweet dishes. There were fruits, glutinous rice – luridly coloured in diverse shades – and various unidentified objects of a worrisome appearance. When a customer materialised she would desist from waving her fly bag – an ingenious device constructed of a fly swat with a plastic bag tied to it that made a whooshing noise when flapped about her uncovered goodies. At once, the flies would swoop down to enjoy a banquet. Unperturbed, she would spoon an assortment of her wares into a small dish, then sit her client on a tiny plastic stool to eat the mess.

Next to the fly-botherer another woman was making the traditional soup that is like Vietnamese pho. Itinerant food pedlars also wandered about the market. But I didn't linger where I saw them setting down their portable braziers. The heat they emitted into the narrow, enclosed market aisles was horrendous. This didn't deter other patrons, who squatted cheerfully on tiny stools and ate the kebabs and other small foodstuffs that the vendors cooked.

I liked this market much more than the one in Saigon. It was even bigger and I found fossicking about in it less claustrophobic. In the rabbit warren of the market's perimeter, I came upon an agreeable young man who, after much pantomime, agreed to make me an extension cord for my emergency lighting outfit. Then I said that I would be back to collect it in half an hour, but, although I hunted for a long time, failed to find him again.

Leaving the market, I contributed to a monk's begging bowl and hired a moto to return to the hotel. This motorbike didn't have a grab bar behind the pillion seat to cling to and at first I was coy about taking hold of the rider, but, as we screamed around the first corner sideways, almost horizontal to the road, I forgot my manners and clutched at him wildly, seizing a handful of shirt. As we blazed around the next corner, I grabbed another handful on the other side and by the time we reached the Renakse I had practically ripped off his top.

The Renakse Hotel is a two-hundred-year-old French building that, with its wooden shuttered windows and tiled roof, looks quite ancient. The grounds are handsome: lush and green with lots of fan-shaped wayfarer's palms, tall, frondy coconut palms and spreading frangipani trees from which myriad birds call. Shaded seats nestle among the lawns and plants in the neat garden areas that are edged by half-metre-high clipped box hedges. Hedges also border the broad drive that sweeps up to the imposing entrance steps that are overhung by the wide, upper level balcony. The curving sides of the steps are shaded by two giant trees and lined with rows of terracotta pots holding bougainvilleas smothered in purple flowers. At the bottom of the steps, a vast ceramic tub of water housed a raft of pink lotus flowers and was also, no doubt, home for the hotel's resident population of mozzies.

My room was on the ground floor at the front of the hotel and the pathway to it led along the wide veranda, the edge of which was hung with clay pots containing orchids in flower. A door on the far side of the room gave access to a tiny terrace that looked into the leafy green garden and was just big enough for two plastic (blue of course) chairs and a teeny table. The walls of the room were panelled with dark brown wood and the ceiling was also wooden.

Extreme age had warped large spaces between the panels of the door that opened onto the terrace, but the gaps had been effectively, if crudely, sealed over with clear plastic tape. Large windows, with wooden shutters and fretwork bars that would keep out most intruders – except those of the insect variety – also afforded a view across the garden. The electric lights looked like an afterthought – the wiring ran down the outside of the walls – and I could see where the original oil lamps had been. The furniture was heavy dark wood, circa 1920, which was when the renovations, including the electricity, looked to have been carried out. The bathroom's concession to modernity was a hand-held shower that, without a proper alcove, splashed all over the room. I had a giggle when I saw that the only lock for the bathroom was a bolt attached to the *outside* of the door. Not exactly a guarantee of privacy.

There was even a supply of toilet paper. Unfortunately I had already learned that, although Cambodian toilet paper looks thick, strong and adequate, the minute it gets damp it disintegrates into a handful of crumbs. But I managed to bang some hot water out of the machine in the bathroom and was able to wash my hair, which had deteriorated into gluey rats' tails. It was bliss to have hot water, even if came from one of those tiny instant heaters on which you manipulate several knobs and forthwith get – but not always – warm water. I had read that Cambodia's water and sanitation system is primitive in urban areas, but almost non-existent in the country and that this is the cause of much disease, especially diarrhoea, the major killer of young children.

A buffet breakfast was served on the hotel's colonnaded veranda and the two terraces that flank the entrance steps. There was fruit aplenty – pineapple, papaya, banana – crusty baguettes that provided crumbs for the waiting sparrows, omelette, small un-naturally pink sausages and delicious strong coffee.

I ate on the terrace from where I could admire the view down the drive to the iron gates, in which the ornate red and gold entrance to the palace opposite was framed. Then, dodging the persistent shoeshine boy and the motos who lay in ambush at the hotel entrance, I jumped in a cyclo and rode along the river. The breeze was reasonably cool as we wafted past the dock where the boats that travel upriver to Angkor are moored. Continuing on, we reached Wat Phom.

Wat Phnom, Phnom Penh's most holy temple, the place to pray for luck and success, squats atop the only elevated site in town. Although the hill whizzes straight up skyward for a long way, it is really just a dot of an uprising, no more than one hundred metres around the base. Crowned with a tall pointy stupa, it reminded me of the Shwedagon Pagoda in Rangoon. The Khmer Rouge murdered most monks and destroyed almost all of Cambodia's three thousand wats, but Buddhism has now been reinstated as the country's state religion. Most people follow the Theravada, the teaching of the elders, form of Buddhism, which came to Cambodia via Burma and Thailand in the thirteenth and fourteenth centuries and was incorporated with the Hinduism that had been brought from India.

Lions and nagas guard the stone steps that lead up to Wat Phnom and near them a sign states:

> *Admission*
> *Foreigners Only*
> *One Dollar.*

I assumed this meant that only foreigners paid, not that only foreigners were allowed in.

I started my ascent, climbing several sets of steep, craggy steps, passing shrines and Buddha statues where people were lighting joss sticks and making offerings. There were no crowds and I was mostly on my own except for the almost tangible smell of incense that pervaded the air. I survived all the flights of steps and came to the final lot that went up, crumbly, broken and slippery, at an ungainly angle. Following a couple of local lads who tripped nimbly up these steps, I tripped after them – and landed flat on my face. The boys turned back to dust me off and set me right way up again.

Leaving my shoes outside, I walked all around the inside of the temple on the summit, alone except for a Buddhist monk who slept, rolled in his saffron robe, on a bench against a wall. The temple was overpoweringly full of buddhas. Dominated by one gigantic statue, hundreds of others stand, sit and lie heaped, packed and piled around it. Most are covered in gold plate or leaf and they all face outwards. Offerings of money, lotus buds and jasmine – threaded into garlands or arranged on a sliver of bamboo – lay before them. I had admired these kebab-like sticks of jasmine in the market, where I saw boys carrying dozens of them, inserted into a bamboo pole, around for sale.

As I left the temple, I passed a terribly crippled man who sat, legs twisted and crooked, on the floor beside the door.

I had intended to do what is customary at this temple and leave an offering for good luck, but I looked at this man and decided that I didn't need luck. People like this poor man make me realise that I am luckier than a whole platoon of them. I surveyed all the money that was already in front of the buddahs and gave my two thousand riel to the cripple. I had begun to wonder about the stupendous wealth I saw in the temples and all the monks who are supported by the largely poverty-stricken community. This reminded me of the Catholic churches in Mexico, whose riches in the face of the general need had shocked me.

Outside, a small boy carrying a cage of sparrows pestered me to buy one so that I could set it free and gain good karma. I had heard that the sparrows are trained to come back again, poor wee things.

I managed to get down the steps on the other side of the hill without breaking my neck. Half-way down I came upon a horde of monkeys jumping about. Several of them had established residency in the hill's spirit house – a spirited enterprise, or had the spirit sublet? Others shinned up and down trees. Some visitors had given the monkeys a handful of bananas and a minuscule monkey, no bigger than the palm of my hand, was managing to devour a banana that was almost as big as he was.

At the bottom of the hill, the elephant that was for hire stood ponderously swinging his trunk. This is the elephant that can be seen from the balcony of the Foreign Correspondents' Club swaying home from work along the promenade at about six in the evening.

A circle made by the junction of several roads forms a ring around the base of Wat Phnom, and Phnom Penh's main road leads out from it in front of a flower clock. Made entirely, except for the hands, of green plants and flowers, the clock covers a large area of ground and really does tell the time.

I was sure that I knew how to make it from Wat Phnom to

the post office on foot and, resisting the enticements of cruising motos, stumbled along the tatty, broken footpath of a side street until I saw a sign that read 'Post Office This Way'. It led down a smaller street where there was no footpath at all, just mud and dirt. Passing a couple of abandoned municipal buildings, I realised that several people were living in one of the two-metre square gatepost guard huts when I saw a man shaking out his sleeping mat in front of it. Later, returning to the hotel at dusk, I saw homeless people setting up for the night on many other streets.

The post office, a big, squarish, French-colonial building is not a patch on Saigon's ornate one. Inside it was merely functional, but at least there was a table to write at. It may not have been attractive, but it was super efficient. Hand-written on a whiteboard on the wall were the days of the week written in French – lunedi, mardi etc. French is still used officially sometimes as well as being spoken by older Cambodians. Also written on the board were all the times that the mail came in from and went out to Auckland, Sydney, Tokyo and everywhere else imaginable. Unfortunately I found that they don't have pre-glued stamps in Cambodia. I had to use an extremely messy pot of glue and a tissue.

While writing a couple of postcards at the desk, I watched the chirping sparrows hopping around outside and wondered what on earth they found to eat. There looked to be only rubbish on the ground. Across the way were two-storey houses made of crumbling bricks and peeling paint. Three giggling girls leaned out from a balcony window. I soon realised that this horseplay was for the benefit of several young blokes who were seated under an awning below the window playing a board game that looked like chess. A completely naked eight-year-old boy came out of the downstairs door of the house and strolled nonchalantly up the street.

Helped by a patient young lady, I sent two postcards. They cost a dollar each – the same as it costs to post a card overseas from home. But the sign by the stamp counter was the post office's best attraction.

Not to put in post:
No Drugs
No Creatur
No Phornography (I wondered if that's the phornography that
   is played on the phornagraph)
No Jewry
No Explosions (how very unsporting of them!)
No Travelling check (well, it would be if it were posted)
Forbids posting of Radio Activ
No Harful Etc.

Outside the post office I commandeered a cyclo and was pedalled back along the promenade, where as the cool of the evening approached, I saw that many men had come out to play the chess game, or to gamble with cards. At the gates of the hotel I discovered that I had only fifteen hundred riel in change and the rider and I had agreed on two thousand. He said that it would be okay, but I didn't want to short change him and a woman selling drinks from a portable roadside trolley – they did that even in front of the posh Renakse Hotel – was happy to change my five-thousand-riel note. Then I bought two bottles of water from her, paid the rider in full and everyone was happy.

The next time I went out I gave in to the harassment of the moto riders at the gate and hired one. Now, I had always pre-sumed that all these blokes could ride – anyone who can even get on the driver's seat of a motorbike is way ahead of me – but I soon realised that this ain't necessarily so. This rider, who looked about twelve, was very, very wobbly. I vowed never to ride with him again. I was always amazed at the way motos would ride blithely into oncoming traffic and manage to get across busy intersections without the aid of traffic lights. This time we did come upon a red light but, what the heck, we went through it anyway. I had a suspicion that the boy didn't know how to stop.

However, I made it safely to the Capital, where the price for a meal was far cheaper than at the Renakse and the serves twice as big. Madame who ran the Capital restaurant was a mature lady, not fat, but a little stout, the only plump person I saw in Cambodia. The only fat dog I have ever seen in all of Asia belonged to the restaurant at the Renakse. He probably got all the leftovers. Maybe that's how Madame grew plump.

While I was eating the Capital bus arrived and disgorged the day's supply of travellers who had been captured at Moc Bai. One was a particularly repugnant European specimen, humping a gargantuan bundle on his back. It was not a back-pack, merely a blue plastic tarpaulin tied up with a piece of string. I caught Madame's eye during our mutual inspection of this unattractive apparition and she raised her eyebrows and smiled.

The next morning I was wallowing in the comparative luxury of the Renakse when my dream of comfortable living was rudely cut short. I was evicted! The smiling young male receptionist approached me and said, 'We want your room today.'

Taken aback, I said that I had booked it for two more nights and asked why I was being summarily ejected. I was told that a French film crew were making a documentary and, because my room was on the front with the most pleasant outlook, they wanted to film in it. He said, 'You pack and move out and tonight you come back.'

Blow that, what about my siesta? Was I to join the other homeless souls in the park? I decided that I might as well move on to the Indochina Hotel, where the people seemed to like me and were an excellent source of information – and their rooms a great deal cheaper. I was being collected from there for the boat ride upriver in two day's time anyway.

I asked the Renakse receptionist for the shirt that I had sent to the laundry. It seemed a hard ask, but eventually, the shirt materialised, complete with the same stains it had left me with and the same dirty collar, but minus a button and looking as though it had been bleached several times. Instead of a nice lemon yellow it was now a dingy beige. However, it had been beautifully ironed. You can't have everything.

Not wanting to lower the tone of this salubrious establishment by exiting in a cyclo, I paid the exorbitant sum of five dollars for the privilege of riding in the hotel car, a beat-up old jalopy with a seat so decrepit I nearly fell through it. On leaving the Renakse, I finally gave in and, contributing to the shoeshine boy's school fund, let him carry my bag to the car. He never did clean my shoes.

The Indochina staff were pleased to see me, which restored my self-esteem. It was nice to be wanted.

At the Indochina my room was shoebox sized, but the bathroom was better and the lighting brighter than at the Renakse and it cost only eighteen dollars. Sour grapes whispered to me that for all the Renakse's lovely ambience and grounds, it cost almost fifty dollars for exactly the same facilities that I'd had in the Capital guesthouse for seven.

My room was, however, rather strange. Where the bed ended the cupboard began. To access the cupboard and wardrobe I had to climb onto the bed. A huge mirror fronted the extremely ornate wardrobe, but the only place I could see myself in it was from the bed – maybe that was the idea. Alongside the bed was a shelf that held a TV and a fan. The toilet required an ascent up two steps onto a throne-like mount, but the toilet paper was in a holder down at ground level. You either have had to bend down to get it on the way up, or stretch down for it once you were up there. Either way required an act of contortion. I had a big window on one wall, but it opened onto the corridor outside and the curtain covering the window was outside in the corridor. I felt as though I was living in a goldfish bowl and hoped that no passer-by got the urge to pull the curtain aside and reveal me in a state of undress. Above my bed hung a large sign:

Be alert
Smoking Avoids of Burning the Sheet Please.
Thanks!

3 Tuol Seng, Security Prison Number 21

The next morning Mine Host procured a cyclo to take me to Tuol Seng, the Prison Museum. This was another place I would have rather avoided, but I was told that it is obligatory if you want to try to understand what happened in Cambodia under the Khmer Rouge. It was a long ride, about five kilometres, but the cyclo rider pedalled manfully. The small canopies over cyclos shaded my head, but I noticed that my feet, despite slatherings of sunscreen, were becoming very brown.

This morning, however, we travelled part of the way under big, handsome trees. Many of Phnom Penh's streets are tree-lined like French boulevards. They are called boulevards too, but have some oddly contrasting names. One is Mao Tse Tung, another Charles de Gaul and, of course, the main road is named for the king, Norodom Sihanouk. Turning off the main road, we sloshed and bumped along side streets full of potholes and mud to reach the prison.

Tuol Seng, the notorious Security Prison Number 21, is now a museum, but before the Khmer Rouge converted it to an interrogation and extermination centre, it was a high school. It must have been a very big school as it covers a huge area. The prisoners who were brought here had committed no crimes. They had merely been declared an enemy of the system. For this they were questioned under torture and killed. The accusation 'enemy of the KR' could be levelled against anyone and for the stupidest of reasons, such as that you were an intellectual, a professional or a city person. Wearing glasses made you an intellectual and many Cambodians were executed solely because they were myopic. Most horrible and incomprehensible to me, the KR killed the 'criminals'' children as well.

Under the Khmer Rouge regime, twenty thousand people passed through Tuol Seng. Seven came out alive. Deaths averaged one hundred per day. Many prisoners died under torture and were buried in mass graves in the grounds. The rest were taken to the killing fields, the extermination camp at Choeung Ek.

Like the Nazis, the Khmer Rouge were meticulous in their paper work – they left documentation of all the prisoners who had been interrogated, tortured and murdered, including foreigners from America, Australia and France. When the Vietnamese army liberated Phnom Penh, seven people were found alive in this prison, fourteen others were discovered dead, still strapped to the torture beds.

I arrived at the prison in time to see the hour-long film that is part of the tour. It tells the harrowing story of one young woman's ordeal. Her thousand-page confession was extracted under torture. Her crime – she was an urbanite.

Few people survived being herded into the country as slave labour. They lived in deprivation and terror. They were not allowed to have any family life, were given little food and were frequently accused, as this girl was, of being an enemy of the state and subsequently arrested and killed.

At Tuol Seng the former school buildings are functional two-storey concrete blocks arranged in a long U-shape. But the extensive grounds around them are filled with wide-spreading frangipani trees, palms and green grass. As I inhaled the perfume of the flowering trees, I wondered if the prisoners had been able to smell this wonderful fragrance.

I had to force myself to enter the buildings. My emotions all screamed, I don't want to do this! The first fourteen ground-floor rooms along one side of the U were the interrogation and torture rooms. I stepped into the first. It was a bright room about four metres square with a large, glassless window covered with a metal grill on the opposite wall. The room was empty except for an iron-framed bed. I could hardly bear to look at the hideous sight of that bed. On it still lay the iron fettles that had secured the victim's feet and the rusty chains that had held the arms. A tin battery box that had been used to give electric shocks rested on the metal mesh of the bed. Beside it lay a flower. This poignant gift, placed there by a visitor in memory of the soul that I felt still inhabited that room, made me feel even sadder.

All fourteen rooms were the same. They have been kept unchanged as a memorial to the person whose body was discovered there and who had been tortured to death as the fight for the city took place. On one wall of each room hangs an enlarged photo of the body as it was found. A truly awful spectacle. The walls of the rooms across the back of the U are covered with thousands of images – all the victims the Khmer Rouge brought here were systematically photographed, often before and after torture, as well as after death. I decided that the perpetrators of these crimes were barely human.

Tuol Seng was a terrible experience and quite beyond my understanding, but like the killing fields, I had to see it.

I returned to the Indochina to recuperate with a cold shower. Afterwards I lunched on the waterfront, then moto-ed over to check out the best hotel in town, The Royal. It was very royal, but very empty, and I was not comfortable there. A legion of idle staff watched my every move. The Royal's Elephant Bar is legendary and it was indeed grand, but I didn't think it had as much atmosphere as the Long Bar of the Raffles in Singapore, which is to me the epitome of colonial tropical ambience. But I did enjoy using the elegant loo.

After my essential siesta, I sashayed up the promenade to suss out the famous Foreign Correspondents' Club. This was more my style. Housed in an old colonial building, which from downstairs looks totally uninteresting – just a cement block – I found a comfortable relic of the past. A sharp climb up a brown wooden staircase brought me into a large room dominated by a massive bar of polished wood. Big leather armchairs were gathered on one side of the bar around a couple of low wooden tables, while the tables and chairs of a small restaurant were positioned under the open windows of the rear wall that looked out onto the surrounding buildings. But the serious action of the FCC took place at its front where an open veranda overlooks the river. Here a row of expat drinkers leaned on the wide stone balustrade that, interspersed with stone pillars, frames the view. I liked the worn, relaxed feeling of this place.

Right now was happy hour and the FCC was packed with customers. I managed to find a vacant bar stool, and, perched on the edge of the balcony with a half-price beer, looked down on the river and the stream of life that passed along the promenade. Many people strolled by taking the air, while others sat on the low stone parapet that ran along the edge of the river under the shady trees. Minuscule itinerant cooking establishments had been set up here and there on the grass, their cooks squatting on their heels in front of a small burner. Pedlars peddled along on bicycles offering cold drinks from iceboxes.

I moved on to one of the many pavement riverside restaurants for dinner. There is no fast food in Cambodia, praise be, but the food that grabbed my attention on the menu was fish and chips. I don't know why. I don't indulge in this gastronomic treat at home. What I was given here was bloody awful, which serves me right. I couldn't even get any proper chilli to jazz it up.

Many beggars accosted me. The children were hard to resist. One little girl pushed a small boy along in a rough wooden cart. The poor mite had no hands and only half his arms, but he smiled happily as he used his stumps to play with a toy motorbike. I was touched. His carer asked me for five hundred rials. I gave her one thousand, telling myself sternly that that was my quota for the day.

I didn't sleep well. I was afraid of sleeping in and missing the boat to Angkor and woke every hour to check that the clock hadn't stopped.

Not surprisingly, I was ready early and in due course was painlessly transferred, by car no less, to the riverside landing. The two backpackers in the car with me were dropped off first at the dock for the cheaper boat, the sight of which made me very glad not to be travelling in it. It was torpedo-shaped and totally enclosed, with no open deck area. Once down inside that vessel you would have had no chance of getting out if it had tipped over, as I heard these boats were wont to do. And yet this was one of the 'fast boats' as opposed to the other option, which was – wait for it – a slow boat. 'Slow boats,' I read, 'sink often, as they are unstable and if they do get anywhere, they take days to do it.'

Mr Tay, my hotel manager, had done well for me. I had, at no extra cost, a VIP seat in the new boat's top cabin. 'More better for dangerous situation,' he had said.

Bless him, the dear man. I hope his pimples dry up.

The airconditioned cabin on top of the boat had twenty comfortable seats and escape from it would have been easy if the boat sank. There was also an open deck area around the cabin where you could sit in plastic chairs (still blue) if you wished. The deck below housed one hundred and forty seats in what looked like a hermetically sealed, potentially watery coffin.

The hostess, who wore Cambodian national dress (a long, close-fitting skirt and a hip-length overblouse) and a steward clad in black trousers and a white shirt, both of whom looked super smart, handed around wet towels and drinks and we were off. Unfortunately a video was turned on soon after the boat's departure. It produced, extremely loudly, a revolting

American film with lots of repulsive language, violence and sex. All the other passengers were Asian, so hopefully they didn't understand it.

Cambodia has 1900 kilometres of navigable waterways and the Mekong River and the Tonle Sap Lake, which covers 7500 square kilometres, dominate the country. The 4200-kilometre Mekong is the longest river in South East Asia. Rising in Tibet, it flows through Cambodia for 486 kilometres before continuing through South Vietnam to the South China Sea. Phnom Penh is 320 kilometres from the mouth of the Mekong, but ocean-going ships can reach it. Cambodia's rivers and streams mostly flow into the Tonle Sap Lake, which is linked to the Mekong at Phnom Penh by the Tonle Sap River. The Mekong's flood deposits are what make the central plains of Cambodia fertile, so proposals to dam the river are a serious worry and China is already constructing dams in the upper stretches that are under its control. The Tonle Sap Lake is one of the world's richest sources of fresh water fish, second only to the Amazon in species diversity. It provides employment for forty per cent of Cambodia's population and supplies sixty per cent of the country's protein intake.

We left Phnom Penh on the wide, brown Tonle Sap River. The city buildings on the bank soon petered out and were followed by grey, wooden shacks that strung along the river's edge for a long way. On the opposite bank to the city I saw the outline of the Muslim village – Islam is a minority religion in Cambodia. Then we sailed beneath the Friendship Bridge, a lofty curving structure that had been blown up in the fighting of 1975 and only repaired in 1993 when Japan donated funds.

After half an hour we were surrounded by open country. Weeds grew to the edge of the brown river water and behind them stood bushes, palms, trees and the occasional patch of maize with browning silks. Every now and then a gilded pagoda spire rose like a beacon of colour above the profusion of green.

Coffee and, finally, lunch were served on aircraft-type trays that held many small containers, one of which was filled with rice topped by a few thin slices of chicken, unfortunately cleavered up, bones and all. All I got was a slice of bone with a bit of chicken hanging around its edges. The tasty peanut sauce made it edible, but I eyed the cakey thing next to it with deep suspicion. It wore a pastry cap like a cream puff, but from under this oozed not cream, but putrid-looking greenish gunk. Still, by this time I was famished and so I ate it. Suffice to say it's not an act I want to repeat. I was offered more drinks, beer or a thimble of wine looking lost in the bottom of a glass. I had water and more coffee, having found from sad experience that alcohol doesn't go well with the heat of the day.

By this time the river had become too wide to see both its sides, but now and then on one bank I glimpsed a village of impoverished-looking houses made of grey sticks, tin and thatch standing high on stilts at the water's edge. And once there was a town with a few stone two-storey houses fronted by wooden boat landings. Around the town and villages grew large plots of maize and bamboo, but there were extensive areas where no sign of habitation could be seen, except for an occasional cluster of two or three hovels and a boat.

Eventually we burst out onto the Tonle Sap Lake and the banks disappeared altogether. Now the sky was leaden and the boat began to pitch and bump. The waters of the lake can get extremely rough, but I managed to stagger down the deck to visit the toilet, of which artefact the boat owners seemed to be inordinately proud. The pamphlet advertising the boat that I had been given featured a glowing coloured picture of the toilet in all its pristine whiteness. 'Welcome,' said the mat in front of this porcelain treasure as I entered. How nice.

Our boat turned into a narrow river that flowed out from the lake. It was lined on both sides with the dwellings of water-living folk, large sampans and houseboats built on rafts.

None was in the least bit imposing, although some ran to the odd potted tree or plant, but they stocked plenty of kids and a few dogs. All the children were naked, which I thought very sensible in this heat. The dogs were small and Corgi-like, but QE2 would have had a fit at the comparison.

We came to a collection of more upmarket houseboats painted blue, red or yellow, unlike the grey uniform all the others wore. This must have been the ritzy area. Occasionally I saw a half-sunken boat being used as a fish-breeding pond. Other ponds had been constructed with lattice and sticks and out of some I saw people hauling good-sized fish. Canoes paddled by, some heaped with fishing nets while other nets dried on houseboat roofs.

I decided that the people here must live on fish. What else would there be to eat? We passed very close to the boats and through the open sides of the sampans I could see women cooking or washing, one swinging a baby in a hammock. The kids waved at us in delight and the adults smiled.

Then it began to spit rain. Everything was grey, the water, the sky, the boats and sampans, but with the breeze our progress brought, it was pleasantly cool out on deck. We came to the landing spot, which is fourteen kilometres from Siem Reap, the town nearest Angkor, along a deplorably bad track. It had recently rained heavily here as evidenced by the quantities of water and mud lying about. I was not collected in a car as I had optimistically imagined. No such joy. But a motorbike materialised, ridden by a bloke waving a crudely lettered sign saying 'Mis Lidia'.

I slithered down a gangplank that was just a slippery plank with no hand or toeholds – and, plonk, went straight into the mud. My custodian and I sloshed to the bike, and my bag and I were loaded onto it. We hadn't progressed far before we heard shouts and yoo hoos from behind. My new you-beaut watch had detached itself from me and landed in the slush. We returned to retrieve it from the policeman who had picked it up and started again, moving dead slowly to negotiate a safe way along the appalling path, both sides of which were crowded with the huts of the non-water-born people. Not as smart as the houseboats, they stuck up out of the mud on stilts, and were mostly a mere platform with a rattan or woven palm roof over it. Some looked so rickety it seemed that it would take only a decent rain to flatten them.

Many passengers had been collected from the boat and now a battalion of motos and the odd car were all trying to go the same way at once, each seeking to avoid the puddles and mud. After a while I stopped looking down at the sludge beneath our wheels – I had visions of myself sliding sideways any minute and ending up in it – and watched with admiration the Cambodian girls riding side-saddle with apparent ease.

4 Temples and Tuk Tuks

From the ninth to the fourteenth centuries the mighty Khmer Empire was a power in South East Asia, ruling from the Bay of Bengal to Yunnan in China. The Khmer left behind Angkor, classed with the pyramids, the Taj Mahal and Machu Picchu as one of the wonders of the world.

According to archaeologists, prehistoric people who resembled the modern Khmers (as Cambodians call themselves) inhabited Cambodia around 1500 BC and, by 1000 BC, they lived in wooden houses on stilts and ate fish and rice as people still do today. Indian cultural influence and the worship of Hindu gods began around the first century AD, following contact with Indian traders en route to China. For the first eight centuries AD, Cambodia was divided into many small states and the majority of the population lived along the Mekong and Tonle Sap Rivers, just as people do now. In 802, King Jayavarman II united the states and ruled the entire country. A long procession of kings followed, with periods of internal strife, wars with the neighbours and massive building programs such as the capital, Angkor.

The Thais captured Angkor in 1594 and the Cambodian king asked the Spanish and Portuguese, who had started making incursions into the region, for help. This was a big mistake. By 1599 the Khmer were fed up with the Spanish, so they massacred the garrison at Phnom Penh. From then Cambodia was ruled by another parade of kings until 1864, when the French, with the aid of a few gunboats, bullied

King Norodom into signing a treaty that made Cambodia their protectorate. By 1884 it was a French colony. In 1941, when the old king died, the French governor-general of Cambodia placed nineteen-year-old Prince Norodom Sihanouk on the throne, thinking he would rule as a French puppet. He did not and after many ups and downs of fortune he is still there. I have it on good authority, from one who has met him, that he is a lovable old rogue. Whatever he is, he is certainly a survivor.

After the second world war ended in 1945, years of strife between various political parties followed, until King Norodom Sihanouk declared Cambodia independent in 1953. During the war between North and South Vietnam, Cambodia remained neutral, but allowed the North Vietnamese army and the Viet Cong to use northern Cambodian territory. This resulted in secret, heavy carpet-bombing programs of Cambodia by the United States. In 1970, while absent from his country, King Sihanouk was deposed and he was forced to set up a government in exile in Beijing. The bombing destroyed huge areas of land, killed thousands of civilians and produced hundreds of thousands of refugees. Then United States and South Vietnamese forces invaded Cambodia in pursuit of Vietnamese communists. The communists withdrew further into Cambodia and soon the entire country was an imbroglio of fighting.

The Khmer Rouge succeeded in defeating the government forces and in 1975, two weeks before the fall of Saigon, they took Phnom Penh.

Angkor was built between the ninth and fourteenth centuries, at the zenith of Khmer civilisation. The people of Angkor lived in wooden structures – only the gods lived in brick and stone – so the houses of the city are gone and only the stone and brick temples remain. But there is no dearth of those; fifty monuments at least lie here. Portuguese travellers reported seeing Angkor in the sixteenth century and a French explorer, Henri Mouhot, was said to have 'discovered' it in the 1860s. At the time of the alleged discovery by the Frenchman, the temple of Angkor Wat was an active monastery tended by one thousand hereditary slaves.

The moto and I bounced along the bumpy, one-car-wide track to Siem Reap, passing kilometre after kilometre of wooden shacks, the occasional plump pink pig or skinny dog, lots of scrawny fowls, some followed by broods of tiny cheeping chicks, and countless naked children. The track was built up a little higher than the marshy land that surrounded it and nothing grew beside it. Piddling slowly along in the open, it was baking hot. After what seemed like an age we came to water-logged rice paddies, some with green shoots just showing through the water and some with half-grown plants. Now there were also banana and palm trees. At last the muddy track turned into a narrow strip of bitumen beside which wooden houses on stilts started to appear. The houses gradually improved until they became spacious wooden kampong houses that stood on sturdy wooden pylons and had thatch or tin roofs. Their yards and the area underneath their pylons were swept clean and sometimes they had a fence. Then closer to the town I saw the occasional stone house.

At the hotel I had booked from Phnom Penh, I was told that there was no room at the inn! I was sent to another hotel nearby, which was an adequate, but boring, cement block. My moto rider carried in my bag, inspected the room and hung around chatting until he had convinced me to take him on as my driver and guide for the next day. By law you cannot trip around the temples alone, you must have a guide – presumably to protect, or account, for you, but I did not realise at that time that there was an alternative to a motorbike.

I did a Goldilocks and tried three rooms before settling for one that had hot water but no air conditioner. Apparently you couldn't have both. None of the rooms had toilet paper. A hose with a nozzle on the end of it issued from a hole in the wall near the loo and, wondering what it was for, I picked it up, pushed the lever on the nozzle and got a face full of water. I don't think my face was where I was meant to squirt it. It was good that the toilet paper holder was empty, because the toilet was once again positioned on a pedestal and the toilet paper holder was down on the floor.

At half past four, when it was marginally cooler, I set off to explore the lay of the land. Walking down the dusty street, I found that I was on the main drag into town and that Siem Reap is small enough to cover on foot. The pavements were just narrow strips raised a little from the wide dirt road. Despite the expanse of road and the sparse traffic, for some obscure reason motorbike riders – who, like all the rest in Cambodia, rode anywhere they darn well pleased – often preferred to ride up on the footpaths and they whizzed around me as I walked along, which was not a little disconcerting.

Siem Reap, which means 'Siamese defeated', did not appear terribly elegant, more like quietly rustic. It consists of a collection of small villages gathered around the French colonial town centre. The Siem Reap River flows through the town, but several bridges cross it at convenient places, allowing easy access to either side. I read that although there are bandits in the surrounding countryside and mines at remote temples, the town was safe enough.

Apart from food, I was looking for a better place to lay my head. I found it at a two-storey villa guesthouse on a street close to where I was currently billeted. In this delightful place a charming young woman showed me an upstairs room and told me that it could be mine for nine dollars. I grabbed it. The room was only fan cooled, but a lovely plant-filled balcony surrounded it and two large windows made it bright and cheerful. Windows are as scarce as hen's teeth in cheap accommodation. I walked further on down the road being accosted, but not unpleasantly, by moto drivers. Like the street sellers, I found that even if you didn't patronise them, they remained friendly. Cambodians seemed to be almost universally kind by nature.

I had a meal at a restaurant on the corner of the crossroads that lead either to town, or out to the temples of Angkor. I liked the sound of the 'wolfoff' salad, but chose to eat sweet and sour chicken, which came with the usual pile of neatly shaped rice served on a separate plate. You are expected to move the other stuff on to the rice bit by bit. It beats me why – bung it all on together I say. However it is not manners to do so. When I left I received a fetching little curtsey and a sompiah from the waitress.

In the morning I woke to see the floor of my room strewn with bodies. I thought that they were just the usual gigantic cockroaches that had cashed in their chips during the night, but closer examination showed them to be five-centimetre long crickets. How they had entered my sanctuary was a mystery, as this room was sealed like a tomb. You couldn't open the window or the curtains.

I washed my hair and availed myself of all the hot water I could. I wasn't going to get any where I was going. Fat lot of good the hair fixing was, three seconds on a moto a little later and I looked as though I had been dragged through the proverbial bush backwards.

As it was still only half past eight, and I had not arranged to meet my moto driver until nine, I doddled around the corner where there were several tiny cafés. Sitting all by myself at a communal wooden table, I tried to decipher the attempt that had been made to translate the menu into English, eventually convincing the woman who was cook, waitress and probably owner as well, that I wanted omelette with bread and coffee, black, no sugar. Wow, it was great coffee again. After Cambodian coffee the instant stuff I make at home tastes like mud.

A mammoth plate arrived loaded down with a whole skinny torpedo loaf of bread. It took me a while to realise that the egg part of the order was hidden under the bread. It was not an omelette. It was two eggs fried together in a solid mass. The eating equipment was brought on next – a spoon and fork and a whacking great wooden-handled, serrated edged bread knife. I pondered over this last implement until I tried to sever the egg affair asunder with the fork and discovered that it had the resilience of rubber. I needed that knife.

As I ate, the noise of moto traffic roared at me from the road, whizzing by, stirring up clouds of dust. An occasional remorque moto chugged past. The motorbike equivalent of a semi trailer, remorque motos are long, narrow wooden carts that look like half a boat and are hooked onto the back of a motorbike and used to move goods and people. I saw one crammed with about sixteen people sitting ranked along its sides, swinging their legs in the air.

Breakfasting in solitary splendour, I watched the cook performing her culinary feats. Under the table on which she cooked on a gas ring I could see a gas bottle, obviously the power supply, and curled alongside it was a little dog that looked like a mutated King Charles spaniel. Nearby, in a cane armchair, a girl sat playing with a chortling naked baby. It occurred to me that little girls here don't need dolls, they have the real thing. There are always plenty of babies around. Here I also saw my first Cambodian cat – a half-grown tabby, it was the café's pet.

I paid for my meal and, collecting my motorbike driver and my bag, went to find my new accommodation – which, of course, I couldn't do. It didn't look the same going up the road as it had coming down, so we passed the guesthouse a couple of times without my recognising it. Finally, stumbling off the back of the bike I said to Madame and her helpers, 'I lost you.'

They, all smiles, said, 'Yes, we saw you.'

It was hard for me to hide in Cambodia. I stuck out like a pork chop at a Jewish festival. What they were probably saying was, stupid bloody tourist. I dumped my bag and offered money. It was refused. No one wants your money up front. Then I was off at last to the fabled temples of Angkor.

The six-kilometre road out to the temples passes a few buildings and an agreeable park, then you are out in the countryside. It was a pleasant ride because at that time of the day the road was shaded for a fair amount of the way. At the gates of the Angkor complex I encountered officialdom in the form of a woman guard with a Gestapo attitude. I tried to hand her the fee for a three-day pass, forty US dollars, and breeze through. But she said, very severely, 'No! You will get off the bike. You will give me a photo.'

Nobody had told me about this. Fortunately I happened to have some passport photos in my all-purpose handbag – you could perform an appendectomy out of this bag. 'And,' she continued most sternly, 'you must carry this at all times. You will not cut it up or bend it or do anything else to it. Okay?!'

'Okay,' I promised. And was allowed through.

From the gates it was still a long ride out to the various temples, which are scattered over jungle-clad countryside. I had, in my ignorance, imagined that you went to Angkor and stood in the blazing sun to look at one great big temple and that was it. But you drive many kilometres between numerous sites, travelling on paths lined by humungous greenery and many trees. Along the way I saw groups of workers cutting the grass at the sides of the road. They did this lawn mowing with machetes and hoes – no ride-on lawn mowers here. Although some trees were very tall and skinny, many others had colossal spreading canopies that gave great shade.

Reaching the first site, I dismounted, and Samon, my rider, left me to do my stuff while he reclined under a nearby tree. Before long I envied him and would have gladly swapped roles.

This place was Angkor Thom, a walled and moated royal city; the last capital of the Angkorian Empire. In the centre of the walled enclosure are the Bayon temple and the Royal Palace. I approached the eight metre high wall that runs for twelve kilometres around the complex and is bordered by a wide moat. Passing through one of the four gargantuan gates that soar twenty metres high, I fell under the gaze of the four colossal faces that, coldly, enigmatically smiling, crown the city gates and, gazing out over the four cardinal points of the compass, watch over and protect the entire kingdom – and give the odd tourist the eye. On one side of each gate stand fifty-four giant statues of gods and on the other there are the same number of demons.

There are more faces in the Bayon, a three-storey high, sandstone and laterite temple that covers six hundred square metres. It has fifty-four gothic towers and the four sides of each tower has a carved face, making more than two hundred pairs of eyes to subject intruders to intense scrutiny. There was no way to escape them. A dozen or more regarded me from all angles as I walked around.

The centre of the Bayon was under restoration and I was not allowed in, but I hiked a long way around its walls. They are covered in wondrous bas-reliefs that show scenes of wars, royalty and everyday affairs that brought the city to life for me. I went back in time to shop with the artist in the market, play chess, watch a cockfight and see a child being born.

At the royal enclosure, I walked along the three-hundred-metre-long reviewing stand that was used for public ceremonies and is known as the Terrace of the Elephants. Once covered with wooden pavilions, its life-sized lions, garudas and rows of elephants now bask in the sun.

The walled city was stupendous. The walls alone are a wonder. In the twelfth century there were no cranes like the one they were using for the renovations.

Finishing my inspection of the complex, I looked for Samon. He had told me to meet him across the way where a collection of shaded stalls offered a place to rest and a welcome drink. I collapsed onto a bench and bought a coconut with a straw inserted into its lopped-off top. Packs of pesky kids lay in wait for unsuspecting tourists at this place and I was soon almost submerged under a wave of small, vociferous pirates, who did their utmost to sell me flutes and other junk I didn't have space for in my bag. I did give in, though, and bought some postcards. I had to buy them somewhere, so it seemed better to patronise these pint-sized entrepreneurs than a tourist shop.

A diminutive brat shouted at me, 'One dollar, one dollar.'

'American dollar or Australian?' I countered.

We agreed on Australian, after I had explained its value. But I had made a fatal error. I had proved that I was not only in possession of cash money, but could, if shouted at enough, be badgered into parting with it. The children remained buzzing around me like a hive of angry bees and although they did not get cross when I said, 'No thanks,' they were utterly persistent and would not go away. I had lobbed there at the same time as a singularly ugly Frenchman and one little girl said to me, 'Your boyfriend bought something.'

'That's not my boyfriend!' I said, with a look of horror on my face, and she went into a fit of giggles. One woman to another, she understood.

Samon eventually rocked up, looking as though he had been asleep. Sensible lad. He drove me to the next temple and sent me in with the usual instructions, 'Don't walk anywhere except on a path, because there are land mines.'

The Khmer Rouge had been here too. They had not only mined sites where people were known to go, but had also used temples all over the country as places of mass extermination. On the ride out from the town Samon had pointed out a pagoda to me that he said had been the killing fields of Siem Reap.

I dutifully obeyed Samon's instructions and did my Good Little Tourist act at this site. We moved on to another temple, but from the back of the bike I eyed the huge walk in the hot sun needed to reach it and baulked. By this time there was not a breath of air and out in the sun, even under my brolly, it was too hot for strolling about.

Back in my room, I had a cold shower and collapsed on the bed under the fan, which I turned up to go flat out, full bore on number five. I slept for more than an hour, then took myself downstairs for lunch at the guesthouse café, which faced the street at the front of the building and was open on three sides, but was protected from the dust of the road by a row of big potted plants. A young man turned the fan on for me and gave me an exercise book in which I wrote my room number and what I ate. When I tried to pay, I was told, 'No, pay later.'

They operated on the honour system and you paid your accumulated bill when you checked out. I chose a dish that translated as chicken and fried tomatoes and was delicious. A spoon and fork, swimming in a large glass of hot water, were produced. I supposed that the idea was to keep the eating irons hot. Just what I needed. The serviettes were housed in a square plastic box, custom-made for the job. It had a hole in its top from which a piece of the paper peeped enticingly. I pulled at this and was surprised to find, not one serviette, but lots and lots, coming out. It was a roll of toilet paper.

During lunch I was treated to a floorshow. A strip-tease no less. In the front courtyard of the villa was an old-fashioned, cast-iron water pump and under this one of the family-cum-staff was taking his bath. Clad only in the kind of undergarment the men seem to wear, a pair of baggy shorts, he sluiced himself vigorously all over. I was distracted for a while and when next I looked he was buttoning on a crisp clean white shirt. Darn it. I had missed the bit where he took off the shorts.

At four o'clock Samon re-appeared as arranged and I leaped onto the bike again. I felt terribly wanton jumping onto a moto astride. Females here always sit sidesaddle when they ride pillion with a man. They ride astride sometimes when two of them are on a bike, but, as most wear modestly long, narrow skirts, this is usually impossible. The monks all ride sidesaddle too. Imagine hitching up those saffron robes to get astride – it wouldn't look awfully chic. There was no way I could have stayed on sidesaddle. I would have been pitched off onto my nose at the first corner.

We rode to the gates of Angkor again, and then trekked onwards, this time to Angkor Wat, the holy grail, the image of which is familiar to most people and is regarded as the essence of Angkor.

I was not disappointed. The biggest and best preserved of the temples of Angkor, Angkor Wat is visually, architecturally and artistically spectacular. Because it is oriented westward to the setting sun, it is thought to have been built, early in the twelfth century, as a funeral temple. Dedicated to Vishnu, it has four protective walls on three levels and covers over two hundred hectares.

Originally common folk, like me, were only allowed as far as the first level – no further than the first wall. Priests went to the second; the third was the sole right of kings and high priests. It takes a minimum of two hours to clamber around Angkor Wat and most visitors go there in the late afternoon to watch the sunset. Others go at dawn, but that was out of the question as far as I was concerned.

Crowds of tourists thronged the long causeway that led to the temple. Most visitors to Cambodia fly in and out of the north and only visit the temples of Angkor. At this time of the year they were mostly Cambodian city slickers from Phnom Penh doing their bit for the travel industry, or visitors from other Asian countries such as Thailand and Vietnam. The odd European stood out in the crowd, looking uncomfortably hot and frazzled. Asian people must feel the heat too and some looked very tired, but they don't get that awful, blotched gasping sweaty red look that Europeans do. I was no exception, but I was the only one of this breed with the good sense to use an umbrella. Many of the Asians had umbrellas, but not the Japanese. They all trotted about in peculiar looking hats.

The massive causeway to the temple crosses a wide, rectangular, water-filled moat that used to be occupied by man-eating crocodiles in the good old days. The huge sandstone blocks that form the causeway are rough rectangular affairs and I had to watch my feet to avoid tripping on their irregular edges. Stone griffins and other mythical beasts flank its sides.

As I came to the end of the long hike and approached the temple, I saw before me the façade that I remembered from all the photos I had seen of Angkor Wat. But I hadn't realised that what you see, isn't necessarily what you get. Behind the façade is a monumental spread that I'd had no idea was there.

The rectangular outer wall, a thousand metres by eight hundred, is richly decorated with sculptures and carvings. Passing through the wide main gate porch, in the tower of which is a three-metre tall statue of Vishnu that was carved from a single block of sandstone, the temple unfolds before you – one amazing entrance after another that lead to courtyards and stupas. The first part is narrow, but its domed roof is as high as a cathedral and way above me I could see the rough stones of its construction. Then, climbing up countless steep steps and walking through many courtyards, I reached the main stupa, in the central sanctuary of which a solid gold statue of Vishnu once resided. The four sides of the stupa are incised with fifty or more steps that ascend to its top, rising almost vertically with very little incline. They were deliberately built this way in order to make worshippers crawl up them, head down, in an attitude of abject humility, paying homage to the gods.

I didn't make it to the top. I don't mind exhibiting a bit of abject humility for a good cause, but my acrophobia wouldn't allow me to proceed any further once I realised that coming back down would be the hard part. I would have to look at that drop under my feet!

I progressed through many courtyards and colonnaded areas, occasionally sitting on a wall for a rest and a drink from my water bottle. At one halt an Italian man asked me, 'Lei Italiana, Signora?'

'No Australiana,' I replied.

'Ah,' he said, 'Ortralia.'

Not the two-dimensional structure I had envisaged, Angkor Wat was so much bigger than I could ever have imagined. It seemed to go up and on, further and further, forever. At one place there was a powerful smell of incense and I found people worshipping before an orange-scarf-draped, flower-strewn statue of the Buddha. In the fifteenth century Angkor Wat had been re-opened as a Buddhist monastery and the two religions cohabit in it still. In another stupa, old women attended long rows of Buddha statues where local people come to pray. A little further on I noticed a girl cutting a long black strand from her hair. She placed it in front of a statue and I recalled reading that young people about to marry leave locks of their hair here to obtain blessings on their union.

Returning to my guesthouse in the dusk, Samon and I rode up behind a man on a motorbike who had a big cylindrical roll of openwork bamboo, like a fish trap, tied on the back of his bike. When we came closer I saw that there were six pink objects squashed in the bamboo basket. They turned out to be round, fat, pink piglets.

In the evening I sat on the wide veranda outside my first floor room enjoying the breeze and examining the construction of the veranda's roof. From underneath I could see that it was made of metal sheets that overlapped each other, but were not fixed together in any way, only supported by metal brackets. But here and there pieces of cardboard beer cartons had been crammed under the brackets for extra strength. The underside of this veranda was home for what seemed to be all the sparrows in the town – from first light in the morning they kicked up a terrific racket. Large, leafy plants in ceramic pots stood on the shiny brown tiles of the floor and formed a screen around the edges of the veranda railings. A plethora of fine, polished wooden furniture decorated the area. There were armchairs, tables and a wonderful wooden suspension rocking chair that I would love to have been able to slip into my bag. My room had no furniture apart from the bed and a strange wardrobe, the front of which was made entirely of glass – not a terribly good idea; my travelling clothes are better hidden from the public gaze.

I walked down a nearby lane to the Aspara guesthouse for dinner. According to my guidebook this enterprise was supposed to have a garden. I sometimes wondered about the blokes who wrote my guidebook. It seemed to take very little to impress them. Are they so used to living rough that two dusty pot plants constitute a garden? It was very, very hot in the Aspara's restaurant and the fan didn't reach me. Three Germans men sat under it, smoking up a storm and giving their driver an English lesson. Poor lad, no one will ever understand him, except maybe another German trying to speak English.

I obtained a decent meal and one of the help came to keep me company. His friend soon joined him and they both watched me eat. I didn't mind this, but I did wish that the one next to me would stop picking his nose. I learned from my spectators that schooling is free, but that some parents can't afford the few dollars required each year for books and uniforms. A few of the little dears from the local school had peddled past me this day. They wore white blouses and navy shorts or skirts.

Just then a portly brown frog hopped onto my foot under the table. Fat drops of rain were plopping down and I guess these had brought him out. A shame there were no more plops – a decent rain might have cleared the air. I had been searching the heavens for signs of rain since this morning, when the blue sky had become streaked with white wind clouds. They later turned to leaden thunderclouds, but no rain came.

At breakfast I watched the plants and palms of the café being sluiced and the ground washed. The breeze was cool, but it was hotter here than in Phnom Penh and it was still only seven o'clock. The traffic had already built up on the road outside and there was a continual honk of moto horns. A monk padded silently up on bare feet to stand in front of the villa, holding his alms bowl before him in an attitude of humility. A small boy was sent out from the family's quarters with an offering, and then, making a sompiah, he knelt to receive the monk's blessing. Nearby his mother was tending the red and gold spirit house that perched on a platform by the water pump. She renewed the flowers and set out wee bowls and dishes that contained offerings of rice and fruit.

Having learned that I could hire a tuk tuk for the day to trip around the temples, I changed my mode of transport. Any alternative to a moto seemed like a good idea to my sore bottom. Tuk tuks are more my style. They are still a motorbike, but they have a small, canopy-covered seat behind them on which you sit in a civilised manner.

On the way to the temples my driver, Nuon, and I passed the Children's Hospital, whose façade sported a sign that, in crudely lettered English, invited passers-by to pop in and donate blood. I would have liked to oblige, but I wasn't game to risk the local needles. I lasted longer on the tuk tuk than I had on the moto, but I still returned at lunchtime utterly exhausted. Although a tuk tuk is a lot more comfortable, I still got bounced, bumped and banged up and down a lot. But it beat the pants off hanging onto the back of a moto, out in the sun.

From my elevated position, perched up on the tuk tuk's seat, which is higher than the rider on the motorbike, I felt like QE2 making a royal progress. The canopy over my seat had a dainty, lace-fringed edge and a clear plastic blind that could be rolled down to protect me if it started to rain. The refinements even extended to a light bulb that swung over my head by a worryingly rough-looking electrical connection. The seat was made luxurious by a piece of foam covered with one of the lovely pieces of cloth that are woven locally. It had gold threads running through a blue and red rosette pattern. Two people could sit in comfort on the seat of a tuk tuk, but I saw up to six Cambodians squashed into them, some sitting on the small shelf in front that I used as a footrest.

We had left before eight. At this early hour there were few people about the temples and it was especially enjoyable on the quiet, shaded roadways. I passed a couple of naked men bathing in the moat and thought how *unnaked* they looked compared to whites without clothes.

'True blue,' the guard at the gate said to me when he read my pass. 'True blue, Ortralia.' He spoke Italian too!

It seemed incredible to me that Angkor had stood for a thousand years and that for many hundreds of those much of it had been abandoned and untended. In places, though, I could see the jungle asserting its supremacy. A seed from a tree drops onto the top of a wall and sprouts, and the roots finger their way down either side of the wall, coiling, curling and gripping the stones, sometimes looking sinister, like octopus tentacles in a horror film.

By the time we arrived at the third temple and I was once more pushed off to do my tourist stuff, I had almost had it. One more of these temples, I thought, and my driver will need a cattle prod to poke me out. I was fed up with climbing countless steps, but, reluctant to bring disgrace on my driver, who seemed to be responsible for my behaviour, I creaked up the first couple of flights. Then, nipping around a column, I snuck to the other side and, disappearing from his view. I had a nice sit down. A lie down would have suited me better, not to mention a cup of tea and a Bex. But there's no rest for the wicked, or the tourist, so it was soon up and on to the next temple.

Two more and I declined the next one. 'No,' I said. 'Finish!' – and refused to go in and do my Good Little Tourist act, even though a mini-bus load of dutiful Japanese arrived and did the right thing, trudging off to face more steps and more temple interiors. I was templed out.

My driver was disappointed that I wouldn't do my bit to get my money's worth, but I promised to redeem myself at the next site. Riding around in the luxury of a tuk tuk on the cool shaded roads was fine; I could have done that all day if my driver hadn't kept pushing me off to examine temples. It was all right for him, I sulked, all he had to do was drive the motorbike and then lie snoozing in the back seat waiting for me to exhaust myself with the real work. I could have taken to the jungle to escape for a while, but I wasn't prepared to endanger my life by ignoring the warnings about land mines. Not to mention the deadly, light-green hanuman snakes that were said to abound in that green haven.

So I had to visit another temple. Entering this one meant a long hike along a dirt path as soft as sand. Halfway along the path an orchestra sat cross-legged on the ground playing flutes, drums, funny looking banjos and an instrument like a zither that produced a pleasing tinkling like that of a gamelan. A short distance away two groups of small boys imitated the orchestra by hitting empty drink bottles with bamboo sticks. In front of them they had placed a plastic bottle cut in half. I dropped a donation into the bottle for their ingenuity and enterprise.

I was almost alone at this temple, which was surrounded by many paths through trees and jungle. It was very quiet as I followed the arrows that signposted a trail strewn with the yellow blossoms that fell noiselessly from the overhanging trees. A lizard zigzagged through the grass beside me, a fine, big dark-brown fellow with a lovely black and yellow stripe down the centre of his back. I came to the end of the path and was confronted by a large cement pond and a sign above it that said 'No Enter Water'. No problem. There was no jolly way I would Enter Water. Who knew how many of those fierce crocodiles were still hanging about?

On the other side of the complex, monkeys hooted in the trees, yellow butterflies flitted among the bushes and wild figs hung down or lay about underfoot. I came upon some children sitting beside the path playing tic-tac-toe, moving a pebble between lines and squares drawn in the dirt.

After this, which felt like my forty-thousandth temple, I called a halt, saying, 'No! Lunch and resting time.'

The sky looked very dark and I felt that, with luck, we might get some rain to cool the air before I made another foray out. Returning to the main gate we passed the station where six elephants stood patiently in a line waiting for customers. To board an elephant you had to climb a rack of iron stairs up to a platform that was built around a tree. From there you stepped across onto the elephant's neck and clambered into the green and yellow painted wooden howdah. The elephants were a very dark brown colour compared to the beige-colour of African elephants. The ticket for the elephant ride carried the caveat that the ride could be cancelled at any time due to the 'Bad Behaviour of the Elephant'. The elephants looked very happy to me. Maybe they were on tranquillisers.

We took another way back to Siem Reap; this time we rode around the perimeter of Angkor. Here the jungle had been cleared and rice grew, some in flooded paddies where the green shoots were just peeping through the water, while ripe crops were being harvested by women wielding flashing scythes. The haystacks that were dotted around the fields were of the same construction as those I had seen beside the road to Phnom Penh from Vietnam. They looked like witches' brooms. A sharp cone shape, they stood on a platform of sticks and had a pole that came out from their centres and pointed high into the air. The cows that grazed by the roadside were the usual skinny animals, but the buffalo were fat and glossy. We passed an occasional dog that looked like a dingo and a couple of small horses pulling carts piled high with hay.

A siesta restored me to almost normal, and I made ready for my next assault on the temples. Waiting for the return of my tuk tuk, I sat on my balcony and watched the washerwoman performing in the courtyard below. She squatted, surrounded by large multi-coloured plastic bowls filled with clothing, on a tiny wooden stool under the water pump. My lemon shirt was in one of those bowls. It had finished its day on the back of a motorbike in almost as sorry a state as its wearer. It had been a mistake to bring this shirt, which was not drip-dry like the rest of my gear.

Before hitting the templing trail again, I asked Nuon to take me to the town market. Situated beside the river, it sprawls across two blocks, divided by a road. On one side of the road is the old market that sells local goods and produce and on the other is the new market that sells touristy objects. Mind you, there were some interesting items there and the goods were well made and inexpensive, but I steeled myself to be strong willed and resist. My bag was just too small. Yes me, with a small bag for once. But I had said that in Brazil and I still came home with a really gross stuffed piranha. I put that aberration down to mental instability brought on by heat exhaustion.

Zooming through the old market, past the 'peg required for the nose' meat stalls where men were whacking up bloody carcasses on trestles, and carefully negotiating my way over the rickety planks of wood that covered the open drains, I reached the market interior. Here women sat on the ground beside baskets and bags of fruit and vegetables, or tended tiny stalls that displayed packets of washing powder, bars of soap and such like. I asked one woman where I could find some elastic, twanging the waist of my pants to illustrate my need. Message understood. I was directed to a stall where I bought a metre of the required substance for twenty-five cents. By the giggles that followed I think I was outrageously overcharged. I was happy though. I needed to replace the waistband of a pair of trousers that had recently let me down in public. The heat had got to them too, I guess, and only the fact that a good nurse always carries a safety pin saved me from making an embarrassing spectacle of myself.

Leaving the market I passed the Dead Fish Restaurant. I guess fish normally are dead by the time you eat them, but who wants to be reminded? I then tried to locate some treatment for my foot, on which, horrors, my plantar wart had re-surfaced. It had lain dormant for a couple of years, obviously just waiting for an awkward moment to rear its ugly head again. I showed my foot to a pharmacist and wrote down 'plantar wart' and 'virus' and was offered Vaseline and when I rejected that, calamine lotion. At another pharmacy things improved somewhat. Here I was offered iodine, but I gave up after perusing the shelves for myself. There was nothing there that would have any effect on a plantar wart. The tea tree oil and Betadine in my first aid kit would have to keep it at bay.

Then it was back to my tourist work. I really enjoyed riding around in the tuk tuk once we left the dust and heat of the town. No wonder my clothes had quickly became filthy and my hair, stiff with debris, stood out from my head like a disreputable halo.

The last temple I visited, Ta Prohm, extends over a large area and is a late twelfth century edifice that has been left almost as it was when found by explorers and is being given back to the jungle. I thought the temple's semi-wild state was lovely. Parrots flitted from tree to tree over my head as I walked through the open courtyards, stepping over stones that had crumbled and fallen. Massive banyan trees invade its towers and greenery clambers over its walls and gates as the temple slowly loses its battle with nature.

As I crept through Ta Prohm's dark corridors, reluctant to disturb their eternal sleep, or sat pondering on its peaceful stones, it was easy for me to imagine that in its day there had been vast stores of gold and jewels hidden here. But it was harder to visualise the temple inhabited by its 2500 monks and six hundred beautiful Aspara temple dancers.

Leaving the temple, I spotted a troupe of monkeys that were out for an evening fossick, scampering around in the grass under the trees.

5 Angkors Aweigh to the Bamboo Train

I moved camp again, to the Aspara guesthouse, whose restaurant I had already checked out. It was almost next door to my recently vacated guesthouse, but off the main road and down a small dirt alley. The room was not as nice as my previous one, but it was much cooler. I had discovered that the windows I had much admired let in the sun and from noon onwards the heat in the room became intense.

I found a lot of buildings named after the Aspara – heavenly nymphs – in Cambodia. It is also the name of the Royal Ballet, which, related to the court dance of Thailand, Java and India, sometimes depicts scenes from the Hindu Ramayana. The ballet's musical accompaniment is provided by stringed instruments like fiddles, as well as drums and cymbals. Early in his reign King Sihanouk released the Royal Aspara Harem of dancers, but classical ballet was still taught at the palace. Few dancers survived the purges of the Khmer Rouge, which killed artists and destroyed culture, but now the art is resurging.

The Aspara guesthouse is a traditional Khmer wooden building and my room was upstairs on the end of a long, wide, board-floored veranda on which a few chairs were sprinkled. There was no wardrobe in my room, but a couple of screws that protruded from a hat rack nailed to the wall proved adequate for hanging my clothes and accessories. Beside the bed was a low, cloth-covered table on which sat a small lacquer tray that held a set of tiny lacquer cups and a vase with three artificial rose buds. A fluorescent light that made an appalling row – like a jumbo jet passing through – was fixed way up on the high wooden ceiling.

The shower was the usual hand-held job that some enterprising person had wired to a hook on the wall. An electric socket dangled out of the wall, swinging nonchalantly on a piece of sticking plaster. That night I tried to plug my hair dryer into it and all the lights blew out. Fumbling around in the dark, I dragged on enough clothes to go downstairs and get help. One of the boys came up with me, flicked a switch and there was light again. Automatic fuse, I guessed. At least they didn't discover that I had done the deed that broke it.

My window had wooden shutters that opened outwards, but no fly screen, only a tatty piece of lace for a curtain. But it was on the back wall of the guesthouse and from it I could see, over the roofs of ancient-looking tiles, down to the yards of the houses below. In the greenery-filled backyard directly underneath me, there was an enormous earthenware jar of water, alongside which rested a bowl, a kettle and some planks of wood under a line of washing. I presumed that this was the water supply and the ablution area. They also had an outside loo, a little wooden dunny that nestled under the waving palms and banana trees.

Quite early for me, I went downstairs seeking breakfast. At this hour I was conscious of that peculiar stillness you get in the tropics, the quiet breathlessness like the world is waiting for something.

I asked Lon, the manager, waiter and general factotum, how I could buy a ticket for the boat to Battembang, the next town I planned to visit. As though summoned like a genie, a gent appeared, produced a ticket for the next day's boat and asked me for fifteen dollars. I told him that down in the town I had seen a sign offering tickets for thirteen, so we agreed on fourteen. He then gave me the bad news. I would be collected at six in the morning. To my enquiry about the essentials of life, he informed me that there was no food or toilet on the boat. This would, I decided, necessitate the restriction of my fluid intake in the morning.

I took a moto to the Butterfly House that I had read about. Entering through a tunnel-like arbour that was completely covered with purple flowering convolvulus, I found myself in an enclosure with fifteen hundred of the multi-coloured, winged wonders. Netting that is so high it convinces the butterflies that they are free encloses the entire grounds. On one side there is a huge, cement above-ground tank that contains massive goldfish. Glass windows have been set in the sides of the tank, so that you can see in, and the carp, presumably, can see out. Shaded paths lead around a garden criss-crossed by stone-edged rivulets of tinkling water that wend among guava, coconut and custard apple trees. Splashes of red, white, purple and yellow flowers are everywhere – vincas, hibiscus, sweet scented jasmine, frangipani and gardenia. Butterflies, some monochrome and some all manner of combinations of black, white, yellow, pale blue, dark blue, brown and red, some one hundred and fifty millimetres across, flit among the foliage. Cool fountains splash into tubs containing tiny, glittering silver fish. What a refreshing change from the oppressive heat outside! No longer hot and dusty, I sank into a cane chair on the shaded patio to sip a coffee in the slight breeze and watch the fish in the tank.

This idyllic respite over, I continued on foot to the market to collect the film I had left there the day before for processing. The photos had turned out remarkably well considering my dismal record with the photographic art. There were only two spoiled shots, but I was given two other photos to compensate – never mind that they were definitely not mine.

I walked further through the town on the pleasant, tree-shaded path that follows the river's edge but is somewhat spoiled by the revolting amount of litter that is strewn all along the banks and waterline. By this time it was siesta and a few people were asleep, flat out beside the path under the trees.

Leaving the town centre, I walked all the way back to the guesthouse, a distance of about one kilometre. On the way I passed many small restaurants and guesthouses, as well as a kerbside mobile mechanic who had knocked off to enjoy his midday snooze in a hammock tied between trees on the roadside. Under him on the grass his tools and spare parts were spread. Nearby slept an old man whom I identified as the bicycle repairer by the pump and tyre patches at his feet. At a petrol station I worked out that fuel was about the same price as it is in Australia. Motos buy their petrol from roadside stands, where murky fluid in containers that look suspiciously like old lemonade bottles stand in a line by the gutter. I was told that the pink stuff is good, the yellow cheap.

I was sweating by the time I returned to the Aspara, but lunch restored me. The waiter was also feeling the heat. He lifted his shirt, and, rolling it up to his armpits, allowed me to enjoy of the sight of his naked torso throughout my meal. Many men, very sensibly, go topless here with their lower half encased in shorts or sarongs. In between looking after me, the waiter sat cross-legged on the serving bench and picked his feet. A friend joined him and they came to interrogate me. I received the first 'You are very beautiful' I'd had in Cambodia. The friend said that this was because I looked Cambodian. He said I had Aspara eyebrows. Whatever.

I was lying down siesta-ing when the bed began shaking. It took me a while to realise that this was not the beginning of an earthquake, but merely someone walking along the board floor of the veranda outside.

In the dusk of evening I went out for a stroll and, coming across a stall with a sign that said 'Business Centre', decided to change some money. The young woman proprietor must have had, by local standards, a lot of money, as she could change twenty US dollars, but the Business Centre was just a canvas-topped stand with a plank bench that served as a desk. Beside the bench there was a wooden sleeping platform with a hammock slung above it. The worker must take her siesta there guarding the loot.

On the way down to the river I passed boys playing foot shuttlecock on the street, and a construction site. There were only a few in Siem Reap compared to the many I saw in Phnom Penh. This structure was only a few metres wide, but I counted twenty-three people beavering away on it. A line of men on the ground were passing up buckets of sand and cement bricks to a mass of folk on the second floor. The ladder up which workers were ascending was a rough device made from two pieces of tree trunk with wooden rungs fitted across them.

I meandered along the river past several bridges and river-side bars that had outdoor seats, spirit houses, ornate gardens and French style lampposts.

Coming back down my alley I was met by a family of ducks out for a stroll. Hogging the middle of the dirt path came the fat mother duck with her four wee babies in tow, all of whom were doing a pretty good imitation of their mum's rolling gait. As I sidled past she gave me a disdainful look and quacked a warning to her brood.

The dinner menu at the Aspara had the usual interesting items such as 'Soap' and 'A Fried Monk' not to mention 'Chicken Amok'. The waiter couldn't tell me what amok meant, but I tried it and it turned out to be not a crazy chicken running around with a cleaver, but chicken pieces in a soup made with coconut milk and spices, and coloured a kind of caterpillar-innards green that was very tasty. While I ate, a scrawny white cat walked casually along the dining table and jumped through the servery hole into the kitchen, probably landing among the food.

I talked to a French woman. I usually found the French aloof. They rarely speak to you in passing, but will respond if you make the first move. Giselle was a travel-ravaged, fifty-year-old professor of philosophy who studies languages. She told me that she always came to Asia on her holidays. When I told her that I'd had quite enough temples, she said that she could *never* get enough temples and spent all her time in the forest with a guide ferreting about for extra ones. I thought this was a bit of a worry, but felt guilty that I'd had enough culture to last me for a while.

Thunder rolled in the south-west and the sky looked very black over there. The waiter told me that rain comes when it's like that. I watched the geckos hunting insects up and down the walls near the light and paid my bill. I had run up a sizable list in the beat-up old exercise book. With total, if somewhat misguided, trust – they didn't know about my appalling maths record – they asked me to add it up. Or did they hope that I would make mistakes in their favour? It was on the cards.

That morning, while it had still been cool, I had re-packed my bag, actually finding the bottom of it for the first time in a week. Not that it was a very interesting sight. Here at the Aspara I hadn't had to worry about the housemaid coming in and playing with my things – the room didn't get done until you left. I hoped that the bottom sheet was washed between clients. There never seemed to be any on the washing line. There was never a top sheet in guesthouses. If you were lucky enough to get any sort of a cover, it was not always washable. That is why it is a very good idea to carry an all-purpose sarong that can be placed between yourself and the cover if the weather is cool enough, or the mosquitos persistent enough, to require one.

Preparing for my six a.m. start the next day, I went to bed early. I stood on the bed to pull the curtain back across the wire it was strung on and from high in the sky the light of a bright full moon fell through the window and shone on my face. A cricket chirped lustily in the garden below. I thought about the fact that not so long ago people believed that moonlight on your sleeping face sent you mad. Maybe I could use that as an excuse for my eccentricity.

Then finally, after the promise of all those gathering black clouds that had come to nothing, it rained, as it does only in the tropics – pouring and thumping down, smacking banana leaves and palm fronds. A chorus of croaking from a phalanx of frogs started up to complement the noise of frizzling, spitting and plonking water. My window shutters banged, but I let them. I was too lazy to get up. Despite the racket I slept reasonably well, and tottered out of bed at five thanks to the small alarm that I had bought one day at a flea market because I liked its colour, not realising that it also lit up when you pressed a button on its side. This had proved fantastic for travelling.

It was good that I was ready early, as Lon was banging on my door at ten to six. Later I realised why the early start had been necessary. It took an entire hour to get to the boat.

I stepped out into the alley that was now a quagmire and both my shoes were full of mud before I made it into the pick-up. When I had been told that I would be picked up, I had not realised that they were describing my transport. It was a pick-up in every sense of the word. I was heaved up into the open back of a small utility. There were already a couple of folk sitting on the wooden benches that were attached to each side and we kept on collecting more passengers until the vehicle was jam-packed full. At one stop they extracted me from the back and rearranged me, a Japanese boy and two Dutch girls in a narrow slot behind the driver. Scrunched in like four parcels, we continued on through back alleys and tiny rough streets.

Although it was early the local people were already up and doing. Women in charge of minute street stalls were preparing to serve breakfast to passers-by, or setting out petrol bottles for sale to motos. We bumped and clumped over the track that led to the boat. It was in the same condition as when I had travelled over it on arrival. A sheet of mud. Last night had been the first rain since then. I was told that this was a drought. Boy, I thought, they don't know what a drought is.

The boat turned out to be an elderly covered motorboat meant to carry about ten people. More than twenty piled in. Someone grabbed my bag and, without comment, carried it aboard, heaved it up to join the pile already on the roof and then handed me some printed propaganda concerning a hotel at my destination.

Three foreigners, a mob of local people and I clattered down a couple of wooden steps into the cabin of the boat to sit, behind the driver and facing each other, on benches either side. Two big Yamaha outboard engines powered the boat from the rear. I felt entombed inside that cabin. If we had hit something or a big wave had swamped us, we would have gone down like a stone – though as my seat was next to the couple of steps that offered escape through the hatch, I might have got out.

The narrow windows down both sides were open and it was very breezy. We had gone quite a way before the second-in-command collected our fares. I already had my ticket, but I couldn't fail to notice that the local people paid less than half the amount that I had. I was seated between two young Cambodians, a girl and a boy, and an older lady sat across the way.

We took off very slowly, put-putting along the river between the lines of houseboats and motley craft of the boat people, passing many sampans going about their business. Two ladies paddled one sampan piled with vegetables from boat to boat making house calls and a man sold cans of drink, groceries and other goodies from another. We pulled up to a barge to collect another passenger. Every time the engine dropped to a crawl I could hear a strange cheep, cheeping. Eventually I realised that I wasn't having delusions – a box of fluffy yellow chickens resided under my seat.

We came out of the river and onto the lake. Immediately the driver put his foot down and we shot off at a great pace, bumping and banging over the wavelets. I saw the young backpacker further down the boat cross her arms firmly across her chest, no doubt wishing to billyo that she had a bra. Even with one it was very uncomfortable.

I had brought food rations to sustain me on the trip and longed to tuck into the baguette the hotel had supplied. I am not accustomed to going without breakfast, but there was no way I could have safely manoeuvred food into my mouth in that chop. Reaching the other side of the lake at last, we turned off it and entered a river and the ride became less wild. Out came my sandwich, which stimulated my elderly neighbour to produce her breakfast – rice in a plastic container in a plastic bag, which she ate with a plastic spoon. When she had finished she calmly threw all her plastic eating equipment out of the window into the river. Others joined in the eating spree, hauling packets from their bags and we all chomped away happily.

I need not have bothered restricting my fluid intake. An hour and a half into the trip we pulled up to a floating house that had been turned into a shop. Tied to its front were crates containing bottles and scruffy looking jerry cans of petrol for sale. The driver of our boat threw a rope over a hook on the houseboat and we passengers stepped across onto its wooden deck, which was piled high with tiers of canned drinks, chips and other munchies.

Two tiny wooden tables and a couple of plastic chairs graced this establishment and coffee was on offer. Once I had established that they had a loo, I ordered a cup. Asking directions to the toilet facilities, I was led out the back and along the freeboard on the houseboat's side. I had always wondered what sort of amenities these boats would run to, but I was not prepared for the shock I received. Instead of the horrible malodorous dump I had expected, I encountered the best loo, bar none, in Asia! A good-sized square had been cut in the floorboards of the tiny cubicle and underneath the hole the clean, green water of the river flowed past. There was no smell, no grot. It was marvellous. Everything was instantly disposed of in the river. There was, of course, the worry about polluting the environment, but I quietened my conscience with the thought that far worse was being done to the rivers of Asia.

Admiring the construction of this Divine Dunny, I saw that one of its sides was the wooden planking of the houseboat that it was tacked onto and the other side was made of old, flattened oil tins. This side even ran to the refinement of a window. A piece of Perspex had been inserted into the tin to provide the occupant with a view of the river.

While enjoying my coffee, I was studied intently by a small mongrel dog and two naked children, one of whom had beautiful, shoulder length, nut-brown curly hair. I would have sworn he was a girl had his nakedness not proved otherwise. Before we left the houseboat, the Cambodians bought heaps of edible rubbish to munch as we continued on, and later, when I emptied my shopping bag that had been sitting on the floor of the boat with its top open, I shook out a pile of chips and cheezels that I had collected from the fallout of the feast.

Underway once more, the driver now had to concentrate hard because parts of the river were narrow and there were many bends where he couldn't see past the dark green foliage, mostly weeds or masses of creepers, that grew thickly to the water's edge. To overcome this, he blasted a dreadful klaxon horn that offended my eardrums at every bend. Even so, we had a few close calls. Before this I hadn't considered the fact that you could have a colossal prang on a river. Now I thought about it obsessively.

Our driver was a young bloke who, apart from spitting out of the window a couple of times (I didn't see a lot of this in Cambodia – maybe because many men are too poor to smoke, even though Marlboro cigarettes are two dollars and local ones are only fifty cents) and looking as if he was going to nod off going across the lake, was very considerate of his fellow river people. Whenever he went past a cluster of floating houses, sampans or other boats moving along the river, he slowed right down. All the sampans were built of brown-grey wood. The bigger ones had square wooden cabins in their centres, but small ones had merely a half circle of woven matting as a cover. On some of these craft I saw people going to market with pigs, ducks or produce. Many large, triangular fishnets hung from the riverbanks, suspended high above the water by the ladder-like poles that they are pulled up on.

Shortly after my young neighbour had pigged out on chips and other non-food, she was violently sick. And she didn't lean out of the window to vomit, she chundered alongside her seat, down the bulkhead, which wasn't the most pleasant thing to be seated next to. Afterwards she took a shirt out of the plastic bag in which she was carrying her goods, cleaned the mess with it, and stuffed the shirt back in her bag. Then she lay down as much as she could on half a seat and, with her head in my handbag, went to sleep. I hoped she had finished emptying her stomach. The older lady opposite me took off her scarf, wound it around her head, draped the end over her face and leaning on the back of the driver's seat, also went to sleep.

After about the half-way mark I began seeing muddy river-banks. Lower down, this river could become impassable if there was not enough rain, but at this time of the year, August, it was sufficiently into the wet season for the water level to be high enough.

Clusters of huts on stilts appeared on the banks, attended by the usual dogs and collections of small children. We pulled into the bank at one place so that a young man could hop ashore and the boat took off again without stopping its engine. I watched the lad trudge up a muddy track that wound around a hill and disappeared into the jungle. Soon after, my chunderous neighbour, now restored to health, also disembarked.

Next we stopped at the base of a high bank, above which was a paling fence painted yellow and green, a popular colour combination in Cambodia. This site didn't look much, but it was Battembang.

Only recently open to land travellers due to the continuing Khmer Rouge presence in the far west, Battembang is the second-largest town in Cambodia and the district around it is known as the country's rice bowl.

I trundled off the boat and commenced struggling up a set of very steep metal steps that ascended to the heavens. Someone threw my bag off the boat's roof and onto the first step. I left it there knowing that some person touting for a hotel would bring it up. A young man did so and I took his hotel in gratitude. He bundled me into a mini van with another couple of waylaid tourists who, to my surprise, began to complain about having to wait. They weren't late for a board meeting, that's for sure. To look at them you'd have thought that they had all the time in the world. Anyone so laid back about washing and tidying themselves would not appear to be the sort to care about a little delay.

In due course our procurer gave up on more custom and off we went to the hotel. It was called The Royal and although it was no palace, it was quite okay. I was given a massive room, easily as big as two of the rooms in the hotels I usually frequent. I fell on the bed and slept for a couple of hours.

Dragging myself out of bed, I climbed the staircase to the fourth floor rooftop restaurant to eat lunch. It was not a fancy spot, but it had no sides so it caught a lot of breeze and was reasonably cool. Brown wooden desks had been placed together to make communal tables for the diners, who sat on wooden or plastic chairs (blue again). Near the edge of the balcony a few wooden lounge chairs were lined up for the purpose of watching the sunset. The tiled floor, decorated with the vestiges of the previous meal, was none too clean. Iron girders supported the thatched roof and a waist-high iron railing, banked with numerous large palms and plants in ceramic pots, kept the patrons from falling off the edge.

I ordered kho phoune which is found everywhere in Cambodia and is like laksa or Vietnamese pho: a big tasty bowl of noodles and soup with lots of unidentifiable objects floating in it. This time I wasn't sure what was edible and what was only decoration. Chomping some of the sticks and twigs and big green leaves that were like those of an orange tree, I found them resistant to chewing, so I desisted. I didn't want to astound the waiter with the sight of the weird foreign woman eating the ornamentations. The kho phoune came with the ubiquitous mound of rice and a plate of lychees, bananas, and pineapple. Everywhere in Cambodia fruit is cheap, plentiful and sun-ripened, which makes a luscious difference to its taste.

The young man who attended me was the only other person in the restaurant. He brought my food from one of several small huts on the other side of the rooftop.

I had finished lunch when a gaggle of rowdy French people arrived in the frazzled state of a white person in the tropics. When the waiter thought we had all been adequately accommodated, he sank into an armchair a metre or so from me, extracted a mirror from a nearby drawer and raked his hair with a big yellow plastic comb. When this part of his toilet was completed to his satisfaction, he picked up a pair of clunky brown shoes, got out the Nugget shoe polish tin and, squatting on the ground, proceeded to give them the clean of their lives. In the midst of these labours my fruit salad arrived and he interrupted his brushing to deliver it to me.

The servery area beside the dining tables had no water tap or other means of washing, just a scruffy wooden desk that provided a home for a CD player and some bottles of water. I would have liked to say 'Would you mind awfully washing your hands?' but didn't know how, so I just tried not to think about this breach of hygiene.

I was the last patron to leave the restaurant and as I did I heard a loud splashing and, looking over to the corner of the roof, saw the waiter now taking his bath, sluicing sheets of water from a stoneware jar over his naked torso with a big blue dipper. I don't know whether he was totally naked – a pot plant was in the way and it's not polite to look. I wondered if all this sprucing up heralded a big night out or if it was merely a daily ritual.

Well fed, I slept again. I couldn't believe for how long when I finally surfaced for breakfast. I ordered omelette with cheese. The latter was a disappointment – a tiny triangle of imported cream cheese formidably encased in silver paper. The omelette was delicious, despite its unidentifiable black spots that I decided must have come from the iron pan or the oil. It had lots of green spots as well. I think it had been embellished with some left overs from last night, hopefully not off the plates. Baguettes are great, but I always made a frightful mess with them, because no matter how careful I am crumbs and crust fly off like confetti in every direction. However, a few sparrows lurked about waiting to clean up after me.

I was pleased to see that my room came equipped with three resident geckos. I hoped they would prove to be a match for the mozzies. There was no toilet paper in my bathroom. Then I spotted it, in pride of place on the dressing table of the bedroom, housed in a screaming blue plastic container with little flowers on it. I moved it to its rightful place by the loo, but the next day it was back in front of the mirror on the dressing table.

That morning I had been shocked awake at dawn by the sound of a wash-trough of water being thrown down the toilet in my bathroom. I was sure someone was in there and watched the doorway apprehensively in the dim light. No one came out. When the noise happened again and again, I realised that my room must be under the rooftop kitchen and that something was happening in the water department up there that was reverberating down my loo.

When I told the hotel manager that I was staying for a

87

week, he upgraded me to a cooler room on the top floor where the loo didn't play tunes. This room had a skinny balcony that overlooked a street, at the end of which I could see the town market surrounded by millions of bikes and motos. The street, like the rest of those in Battembang, apart from a couple of the main ones, had a rubbish-littered dirt surface.

I had hired Dara, the young man who had brought me from the boat yesterday, to take me out for the day on his moto. There is no other way to get around Battembang. First I asked if we could go some place where I could buy a hat, as we would be travelling long distances in the blazing sun. At a roadside stall I was crowned, amid much hilarity, with a stupid-looking cotton affair that was shaped like an inverted flower-pot. It didn't give a lot of shade, but it kept my hair out of my eyes and covered my head. Cambodians don't wear those really useful conical straw hats that the Vietnamese do and this monstrosity was apparently the current fashion. Dara and I took off on a supposed twenty-five-kilometre ride that felt more like twenty-five thousand on his small uncomfortable Honda.

First we rode through the town centre, which consists of a few imposing French colonial buildings, a couple of impressive wats, a row of French colonial shop houses along the river that runs through the town centre, a railway station and a museum. I asked Dara why mobs of police, youths leaning on motos and crowds of men surrounded the outside of one shabby building. He told me that this was the high school and that today the final exams were in progress. The police were there to stop anyone getting the answers to the exams to the pupils. The men and boys were there trying to outwit them.

When Dara had done his final exams, because he was thought to be clever, he'd had to fight off one of the examiners who tried to steal his papers to sell to another student. He said that corruption is found in everything, everywhere, and that the reason there is no money for schools is that, although the government is given aid money, it won't spend it for the people. I had read that more Cambodian men than women are educated and that literacy rates are only around sixty-five per cent for adults. There is a lot of catching up to do since the Khmer Rouge declared education to be evil and killed all the teachers they could find.

Dara confirmed what I had read. That today Cambodia is economically and politically in a very bad way. The large areas of agricultural land that are still mined limit food crops. Aid parcels are sold and aid money syphoned off. The government is shaky. Corruption is rampant and intimidation and murder of anyone opposing them still occurs. United Nations soldiers with money to pay prostitutes began an AIDS epidemic which is among the worst in Asia. Although the average Cambodian is honest, even some doctors, nurses and teachers demand bribes. School tests are sold. The police and military moonlight as armed robbers.

We hadn't gone far when my wonderful new hat blew off and was given a dirt christening. As soon as we left the main street there were only rough lanes and tracks, which became progressively rougher as we came to the countryside. At one stage we rode along what was laughingly called the main road, a metal highway of sorts, horribly potholed and disagreeable to the sensibilities, but it *was* slightly wider. In places where it forded culverts over water, the road had eroded until only a thin strip remained in the middle and the bare iron reinforcing bars of the viaduct could be seen like the bones of a rusty skeleton, not something you'd want to travel over at night.

Shortly we were out among mango trees, rice paddies and animals. We passed many carts, one or two of them horse-drawn, but most great, lumbering wooden hay carts pulled by oxen. The cows in the fields looked in fairly good condition and one statuesque group of geese waddled regally along the edge of the road. The only other mechanical traffic, apart from one dilapidated wheezing truck, was bicycles or motos.

When we arrived at the foot of the very high mountain on the top of which squatted Sampeau, the temple Dara had brought me to see, he told me a Cambodian joke.

What do you call a man standing on the edge of a mountain? Cliff.

Oh dear. A fortnight joke. Too week.

This mountain had been the government's front line in the defence of Battembang against the Khmer Rouge. From Crocodile Mountain across the way, the Khmer Rouge had lobbed shells at the government forces here. On the mountain-top, close to the temple, a couple of field guns remain, still guarded by mines. The Khmer Rouge took Battembang in 1994, occupied the temple, turned it into a prison and used the nearby caves in the mountain as a killing field. In 1997 Leng Sary, Brother Number Three, defected to the government here with all his troops and now, after many years of guerrilla activity, this area is finally safe to visit.

I surveyed the peak of the mountain that went skywards perpendicularly and said that I didn't fancy climbing all the way to the top of it. Dara suggested we go up a sidetrack on the moto. We didn't get far before I called this lark off. 'No way, José,' I said, having visions of the return ride down that nasty steep track that was all stones, dirt and holes. Even riding up it was hazardous. If we had stalled, we would have found ourselves flying backwards downhill at a great pace.

I hopped off and sat in the dust under my brolly while Dara took the bike back to safety. When he returned we trudged up the dicey path that became steeper and steeper with less and less dirt, until it was only rocks and stones. At last we reached high steps cut in the rock and we continued, panting and puffing, climbing ever upward on the steps for a long, long way until finally we made it to the pagoda that stood on the very edge of the mountaintop looking out over the countryside.

The pagoda is very old and holy, but that had not stopped

the Khmer Rouge using it as a prison for the intended victims of the nearby killing fields. Some prisoners died under torture in the pagoda, but most were taken to the deep caves close by and thrown down. The severity of your crime decreed where and how you were killed and how much you were tortured.

Dara and I sat on the edge of the pagoda's concrete veranda to rest. Gazing out at the beautiful view over the lovely land, it seemed impossible to believe the terror that had happened here. Dara told me how the Khmer Rouge regime had affected his family. His father had been a jewel merchant, but when all private enterprise was stopped, especially the sale of gems, which the Khmer Rouge used to finance their war, Dara's family were driven out of Battembang with the rest of its population. They survived the forced labour on the land, but remain very poor subsistence farmers. His grandmother and one aunt made it to a refugee camp on the Thai border and were re-settled in the USA.

During the week Dara lives in Battembang with his married sister, but goes home to his village on the weekend. He gives his family twenty-five dollars a month, which is a large portion of the money he earns. He told me that his family's house cost eighty-five US dollars to build and that his family consists of four children. His mother's family had eight and his father's nine. Cambodians can still have multiple wives, but now birth control is being advocated. I believed this. In one village we had passed through I had seen children blowing up condoms and using them as balloons.

Dara told me that the chanting I had been able to hear from halfway up the mountain came from the monks praying for rain. The festival of the rainy season, which also celebrates the Buddha's enlightenment, was beginning. It was nearing mealtime for the monks, who can't eat before midday and I watched villagers climbing up the mountain bringing offerings of food. The monks, preparing for their meal, were having a swab-down in the temple courtyard. I averted my eyes from

91

the sight of their saffron robes flapping about in the breeze, to watch a mass of black cloud building in the western sky. I hoped the prayers were working. The country people were desperate for rain. Dara said that his father had planted corn fifteen days before, but it had died because there had been no rain since then. In Cambodia this is a long time to remain dry.

A short distance from the temple are the caves where the bones and skulls of countless murdered Cambodians were found. The executioners took their victims to the openings of these caves that descend way down into the centre of the mountain and either bludgeoned them to death, tied their heads in plastic bags, or stabbed them with bamboo slivers, before throwing them into the depths. Some were simply securely bound and thrown down alive.

I entered one cave that contained a large wire-mesh cage full of skulls and bones. The cage was locked to prevent the bones being removed to hide the crime. Beside the cage was a Buddhist shrine decorated with candles and flowers. Dara did not come with me, but he told me that he felt it was necessary not to forget what had happened here.

I had to climb down many steps to reach the dim bottom of the other cave that is open to visitors. Here a very large Buddha reclined, attended by a praying monk. These beautiful caves were so peaceful now that it was hard to imagine that anything so awful could have happened here. And when I thought that all of these murdered people had, like all the other victims, committed no crimes, I felt infinitely sorry for them.

Lunch, and a rest back at the Royal at siesta time, came next. After all the sleep I'd had in the last twenty-four hours I was starting to think that I'd been slipped a Mickey Finn, but now I felt very chipper again. A terrific breeze blew across the lunch table and almost swept it clean of its accoutrements. I put my sunglasses down and they blew straight across the table and into the lap of a dishy Frenchman, who smiled at me so nicely I would have liked to chat him up. But Horse Face, his wife, gave me the fish eye, the old bat, and I don't tangle with wives if I can help it.

At three Dara and I took off again. This time we followed the river along the edge of the town; not a very attractive drive, there was no grass or trees to relieve the dryness. But once out of the town the ride became pleasurable. We tootled along shaded lanes and breezed through villages that were strung along the road. Then we hit the horribly potholed and rutted main road that again consisted almost entirely of lumps of metal, stones and rocks. But a dirt track had been worn beside it and Dara opted to take this smoother route. This time we headed in another direction and travelled through expanses of rice paddy, interspersed with small villages, for twenty-six kilometres.

The further out we went, the more the kids screamed with delight at my foreign face. There were lots and lots of kids. No sign of the population control working here. Then the path led us to the River Sankar and we rode beside it for a distance. The banks were still high and would be until the rains came again. There were a few boats, but no one lives on the river here. The water was much cleaner and wider than in the town, but it was still slow flowing and a murky green-brown colour.

Soon afterwards we passed a large chook farm. It looked rather strange, as it was raised up off the ground on a long platform supported on poles in order to keep the nasties from the hens. But these lucky fowls enjoyed much better conditions than poor battery hens. They were housed in several four-metre-square cages that were enclosed by wire netting and covered by palm thatch. We also passed many cows, buffalo, a big wooden cart jolted along by two hefty, slow-plodding bullocks and a small cart drawn by a petite, fine boned horse. Stands of fruit trees rimmed the villages and peanut patches and a bush that looked like a small flame tree grew around the vegetable plots. This bush has thorns and acts as a deterrent hedge, as well as having edible young shoots.

Dara showed me dragon fruit trees that were hung with long skinny green fruit that turns pink when ripe. I found this fruit, with its white flesh studded with black spots, intriguing and secretly thought it would be more fitting to call it Spotted Dick.

Dara also talked me out of my desire to take the train back to Phnom Penh. He said that the train is hot and hideously overcrowded and has broken seats with no numbers. You can end up standing for hours. It is also dangerous, falling off the rails – often. None of that put me off. But he also stressed that as a lone tourist I would be certain to be robbed. 'Not only poor people, but also bad people, ride on trains,' he said.

Everyone else I spoke to confirmed these less than salubrious facts, so I reluctantly abandoned the idea. As consolation, Dara said that he would take me on the bamboo train later this day.

We reached our destination, Wat Banan. Located in a lovely setting high on a hillside, this is a rather decayed tenth-century temple that resembles, but is older, than Angkor Wat. I got off the bike and surveyed the trillion or so steps that led up the mountain to it with a jaundiced eye. The massive sandstone staircase ascended upwards to disappear into the jungle that completely covered all sides of the mountain. Flanking the steps were huge, naga snake balustrades that looked mysterious as they and their attendant dragons slithered into the lush greenery to be lost among the clouds. Five stupas that were said to resemble Angkor (but unlike Angkor, were really lost in the jungle) reposed at the top of the steps. I took their word for this. I didn't get to the top, deciding to turn back after I'd laboured up a few hundred steps to where an amiable old monk sat smiling and looking hopeful of a donation. I could see the outline of the temple perfectly well enough from ground level.

At the base of the temple a few optimistic drink sellers lurked under thatched roof platforms, but I was the only pilgrim present. Dara and I sat on the edge of one platform and were entertained by a pile of enchanting children who had gravitated to us. One little boy kept putting his hand out towards me and saying, 'Bike bike.'

'I'm not giving him a bike,' I said, but Dara said that 'bike' meant pen. This tot was no more than two and I couldn't see him learning to write before he lost my precious pen, so I gave him a picture of some flowers that I found in my bag instead. That shut him up. The children were fascinated with my guidebook and looked at all the photos for a long time.

I bought Dara a drink, the second for the day and he told me later that people don't usually do this, but he was very grateful. Cokes cost a good deal less out in the country than in tourist places. Coconuts, my choice of drink, were also much cheaper.

Back on the moto, we crossed an extremely long, wobbly, open-sided suspension bridge. High over the river we swayed and bounced on the rattling planks that moved alarmingly underneath us. Safely on the other side, we rode on. By now the sun had almost set and it was really lovely passing gently through little villages where the kids rushed up shouting and waving.

We came to the railway siding where the bamboo train stood. This train is used as transport between villages and I thought it was absolutely fabulous. A wonderfully simple concept, it consisted of a raft-like platform of bamboo slats on a light metal frame fixed to train wheels. Its method of propulsion was a diesel motor, the size of a small outboard, stuck on the rear.

Another two moto riders, who were chauffeuring a French couple, joined us and we all scrambled onto the train. The bamboo train can take four motos and several people and cost one dollar twenty-five for Dara, the bike and me. I sat on the platform with the French couple and the riders hoisted their bikes aboard and sat on them. It was the greatest ride. We went clackety-clacking along at about ten kilometres an hour, which is only half as slow as the regular train. Then I realised that there is only one train line, a single one, a metre wide. 'What if the train comes along while we are out here playing on its track?'

'No problem,' The boys said. 'The train comes up from Phnom Penh one day and goes back down the next.'

'But when?' I persisted.

'No one can tell. It takes anywhere between fourteen and twenty hours. No one knows when it will come along, but the bamboo train is light and we will all jump off and lift it off the track until the train passes.'

'But we are making such a racket we might not hear the train coming up behind us!'

To which came the calm reply: 'That's okay, the Phnom Penh train is so slow you can walk alongside it, plenty of time to see it coming.'

This was when I discovered one of the reasons the train is so dangerous. Because it stops every five or ten kilometres, it is easy for bandits to jump on, rob you and jump off, even when the train is moving. That did it for me. I had read that although the train is primitive, it is ridiculously cheap at less than a cent a kilometre. Until recently it had offered the dubious morale booster of a tin-roofed, armour-plated gun carriage with shooting ports in its sides. As well, the first two flat-bed carriages acted as mine sweepers. A ride on the first carriage was free, the second was half price. Only a fanatical bargain hunter would take up these options. Now the train is merely provided with a soldier and an AK-47 to keep you company in the carriage. I heard about a Frenchman who had recently boarded the train in Battembang, but became so frightened he got off half-way to Phnom Penh.

I enjoyed my ride on the bamboo train so much I thought

that I wouldn't have minded going all the way to Phnom Penh on it. We swanned along tranquilly in the soft pre-dusk evening. The track was built high above the rural land and as the sun cast out its last remnants of glinting gold, the rice paddies lay gilded beneath us. We passed through a couple of village sidings where we were hailed like a royal tour by cheering, waving villagers. After travelling about twenty kilometres through the delicious balmy air, it was back on the moto for the last leg into town. At least my rump had had a brief respite from the battering it had received all day. Motos are only 100 cc bikes and they have a crummy little passenger seat that is not meant for long distance travel. Certainly not over bumpy roads.

It was way past dark when I arrived at the hotel. Dara's fee for this long day was fifteen Australian dollars, but I paid him more. He'd certainly earned it. Early on he had asked me how old I was and was astounded that someone so ancient should be travelling in the manner I was. Thereafter he took special care of me, encouraging me on by telling me how well I was doing and how amazed he was that I could leap up mountains and onto the back of motos when it was quite obvious that my use-by date was coming up – soon. I got the distinct impression that most Cambodian women are dead by my age. They have a hard life. Then I told him that I had a crook knee and he was even more impressed. He said I was wonderful to do this without all my parts in complete working order. At least someone thinks I'm wonderful.

I ascended to the roof for a huge plate of fruit salad and a baguette. A beer, which I hadn't asked for, was plonked in front of me before I had even sat down. I must have looked as though I needed it. I was pretty grotty after all that time on the moto in the dust, but on the stairs I had met someone who looked a million times worse. This American man's face was completely covered with dirt.

'You've had a hard day too,' I said.

'I've just spent ten hours riding a bicycle through dust storms,' he replied. More fool him.

By the end of the day Dara and I were firm friends. More than eight hours on the back of someone's Honda sees to that. Crikey, we were almost related. This back-of-the-moto business gives you a real feel for the countryside, not to mention a smell and a taste. I also had a fair amount of the countryside in my eyes and a heap of it in my hair. When I washed it off in the shower the pile that collected on the floor could have sustained a small rice paddy.

6 Doctor Evil and the Wild West

My room at the Royal had a TV and Sky Channel, whatever that is. Fiddling with it, I came across the 'explicit' station. And it certainly was. But I was soon bored with that. It was like watching someone else eat a meal – not a lot of fun.

It was another great morning on the cool, breezy roof and during breakfast I talked to the French couple, Emile and Sophie, I had met on the bamboo train. They told me that they had not been feeling too flash yesterday. The day before that, in Siem Reap, they had met a retired French Foreign Legionnaire who ran a restaurant with his Cambodian wife. They had imported lots of French beer from Corsica, but no one would buy it, so he had invited my friends to help drink it. They had apparently done their utmost to oblige.

Up until now I had believed that the French Foreign Legion was extinct, but Emile told me that it is alive and well and living in Corsica, which is, along with French Guiana – the former home of Papillion – their headquarters.

After breakfast I walked around to the Chary Hotel. It is the Royal's competition, but it is not as good. It had long, narrow, rabbit-warren corridors that were stacked high with the morning's exodus of rubbish. The rooms were furnished in much the same way as the Royal's, but they were smaller. On the rooftop restaurant, a terrific gust of wind blew the sugar container, a screw-top plastic jar, off the table and its contents spilled all over the concrete floor. The waiter scraped up the sugar with a spoon and scooped it, along with ample dirt, back into the jar. Then he put it back on my table and gave me a lovely smile. I swore off sugar, possibly for life. I know this happens, but do they have to do it before my face?

Having decided that this would be a rest day for me, I spent the remainder of the morning strolling around the town and investigating the old French colonial shop houses along the river. To my relief no one badgered me to buy. A large sign advertised a lottery, called 'Sheepstakes'. I supposed the prize would be a merino or two. Soon it became too hot for promenading, so I holed up in the Royal.

In the evening the hotel manager hijacked his sister-in-law, Any, and her baby girl, Nana, to escort me to the market. We visited a friend of Any's jewellery stall. Fantastic sapphire and ruby jewellery abounded and, although the stalls that sold it were primitive, it was probably genuine, given Battembang's proximity to Pailin, the home of the gem mines. Two beggars approached me in the market, but I had already given my quota for the day, so I didn't oblige. But turning around I saw Any give them each a thousand rials. Later I asked her, 'Do you always give to beggars?' and she said, simply, 'Yes.'

I was up at six next morning, waiting for the share taxi I had organised to take me out to Pailin. This small town, eighty kilometres to the west of Battembang, is thirty kilometres from the Thai border, which is not open to foreigners. The timber and gem resources of the area around Pailin were the financial mainstay of the Khmer Rouge. It was also from here that they launched attacks on Battembang and the surrounding district. The final collapse of the Khmer Rouge came after they lost control of the region and consequently the money to continue fighting. It is now a semi-autonomous zone in which the Khmer Rouge can seek refuge and avoid the law.

Share taxis take the place of buses between towns in Cambodia and they usually carry six passengers plus the driver. Four people in the back of a Caddy or a Buick might be acceptable, but in the small Toyotas used here, you are incredibly scrunched up. And two people plus the driver in the front means two in one bucket seat, which is unbelievable. To avoid doing sardine imitations, you can pay for two seats, which still only costs a few dollars. I had negotiated a price for my share of the car that ensured only three passengers would sit in the back seat. The driver put four in anyway.

The car was a Toyota Camry that looked fairly new, but its looks belied the state of its suspension. It had very little left in the way of springs or shockers. We picked up three Cambodian people. I sat beside the window, a woman sat next to me and a dorky teenage boy clambered in the other side. A gent in a spivvy black fedora hat took possession of the front. One street further on we collected an olive-green uniformed soldier carrying a very large gun. Spiv got out and crammed into the back seat. Suited me fine, I didn't want an AK-47, possibly loaded, possibly with a dodgy safety catch, bumping about in the back with me. I hoped he was on our side. Talk about riding shotgun.

Battembang is not a very big town and in just a few minutes we were in a rural setting of rice paddies that had nothing much between them except the occasional poor-looking village of wooden houses. Now and then there would be a house that looked halfway decent and one or two large houses, though still wooden, stood on estates that probably belonged to the robber barons who were pillaging the trees. Along the way I saw much evidence of logging and we passed many bullock carts piled high with logs. They were not big logs, only fifteen centimetres maximum in diameter, but they were green, straight and very long – young rainforest trees. The road was unbelievable. And the driver threw his car at it, crashing into ditches and holes big enough to bury a rhinoceros, with no thought for his poor passengers. Cambodians, like all Asian people in my experience, especially women, get sick or go to sleep as soon as they are on any moving vehicle and my companions were no exception, for which I was eternally grateful. When Madame needed to throw up, the car was stopped and for a while I was relieved of the jolting.

We passed few vehicles, and they were mostly motos, but I did see a couple of the pick-up trucks that are used to transport goods and people, usually together. One had a small canopy and a bench for the passengers, but the other's centre was packed solid with sacks of rice and the fourteen people it carried were perched around the edges looking most uncomfortable. Vehicles here must have a hard, short life, I decided. Motos often performed the job of trucks and were loaded to the gunwales with goods.

We stopped at one petrol station where a sign announced that petrol was sold by the 'litter' and I watched with alarm as a moto driver filled his tank. He selected a bottle of petrol from a line of containers that looked like rubbish tip salvagees, all the while puffing on a cigarette that dangled from his mouth. When he threw the still burning butt onto the ground, I became anxious to leave. Another moto pulled in. It had a gargantuan rattan pannier attached to each of its sides. On top of the panniers loomed huge sacks of peanuts in string bags and across the back of the lot more bags were tied. The rider had only just managed to insert himself among all this cargo and when he stopped he had to prop the bike up with a stout stick he carried for this purpose.

We came to a narrow bridge where a cow stood squarely blocking our path. It had been tied to a post at our end of the bridge and had wandered out onto the bridge. The cow couldn't go any further because of the length of the rope and it certainly wasn't coming back towards us. Our driver stopped the car, untied the cow and set it loose. That's when I, born on a farm, decided he wasn't a nice fellow.

Soldiers stopped us at several roadblocks and money needed to change hands to facilitate our progress. As well as demanding money at checkpoints, soldiers are said often to tell foreigners that they need protection – and if you are unconvinced they will slip off the uniform and do a spot of banditry.

At one stage the road became slightly better, but this was an even worse worry because then our driver flew along like a bat out of hell, zooming like crazy on this dirt road with rocks and metal all over it and rocketing around blind bends on which the car skidded horribly. I imagined us slewing out of control and rolling over, or crashing into something coming the other way. We were making so much noise with the 'Someone Standing On The Cat's Tail' music that blared from the stereo, that a car horn warning of an approaching vehicle would not have been heard. Bones shaking, teeth rattling, I clung grimly to the door handle as we bounced and jarred along; the dork, the spiv, Madame and I, all rolling around together in the back seat like jellybeans in a jar. Most of our external body parts got intermingled at various times and dust poured in through the open windows to choke us. My hairpins all shook out and my hair fell down.

On arrival, after an interminable three hours, I climbed out looking thoroughly disreputable – a fair match for Pailin town from what I could see, though no one looked as villainous as our driver who was a comprehensively bad looking affair.

Pailin was a big disappointment to me. I had expected to see the Wild West and old Khmer Rouge villains sitting about outside saloons looking evil, but it was just a strung-out line of shanties and hovels. The place was overrun by karaoke dives and gambling was rife. I soon discovered that the guesthouses here are mostly brothels, so I was glad that I had decided to only make a day trip. The one ritzy hotel, a square stone box with over-the-top added decoration and the usual excessively ornate gate and fence, was abandoned. Doctor Evil, as I had named my driver, with whom I was now thoroughly disenchanted, told me that this had been a good hotel, but it had closed due to lack of patronage. Walking along the street,

I peered into the face of every man who looked old enough to be ex-Khmer Rouge and wondered if he was a mass murderer. It was a strange feeling.

I stopped at a café for coffee, but no food was available. Doctor Evil followed me and sat down at the table. I couldn't get rid of this bloke. He offered to be my guide and take me around and, as there seemed to be no other means of transport, I agreed. He said he spoke English, but I soon discovered that, although he could speak a little, it was parrot fashion and he really didn't understand any at all. Nothing I asked him got a response.

I negotiated a price with him that included driving out to have a look at the Thai border. On the way I saw an old field gun rusting in the paddy, many massive bomb craters and the evidence of horribly extensive logging. Entire mountainsides were smoking ruins of burning stumps, denuded, desolate and sad. Rubber had once been Cambodia's primary export, but now the plantations of the north and east produce little and timber is the number one commodity. Although the official revenue from timber is only twelve million US dollars, illicit earnings are estimated to be $184 million. The cash-strapped and dishonest government and military illegally sell logging rights to foreign companies that are stripping the primary forests. Almost all Cambodian forest, over seven million hectares, is allocated to someone, even the national parks and reserves. No tree is safe in Cambodia.

Logging is a major threat to the ecology. The rain washes the soil from the bare mountains and it ends up in Lake Tonle. The silting up of the lake, added to overfishing and pollution, does not auger well for the future.

I could see that gemstone mining still occurred here. We passed many areas of land that were covered with heaps of dirt and diggings, but I had read that it is no longer the operation that it was in the boom days. Rattling over a suspension bridge made of sticks and planks which wobbled something frightful, we reached the border. Right on the boundary of the two countries squat a couple of hulking great casinos, accompanied by a row of seedy, single-storey motel units that function as brothels. The Thais own all this decadence. They have provided it for the edification of their countrymen, who flock here to gamble and debauch. Pailin, which was once a Khmer Rouge model town, is now a den of vice and iniquity.

I finally managed to convince Doctor Evil that I needed sustenance. I was getting desperate. I hadn't had breakfast yet. He kept trying to push me into the casinos and was most disappointed when I wouldn't co-operate. I stood firm, insisting that what I wanted was food, not gambling, at eleven o'clock in the morning, thank you. So he gave in and took me to a place that eventually served lunch. It was a real tourist clip joint that catered to Thai visitors, not the locals. The food took forever to arrive, but while I was waiting a polite young waiter brought a book to my table and asked me to help him with his English lessons. I had never thought about this before, but how do you explain to someone what a word like 'loud' means. You can't say that it is the opposite of soft, because how do you explain soft? I had much difficulty with this and I still wonder what that poor boy went away thinking loud is. A delightful lad, he said that he had been working in Pailin for five months, and I was only the third Westerner he had ever seen. I could understand why. There was absolutely nothing there for a traveller. It was hot, dusty, dreary and not in the least bit interesting. The food I ate was expensive and not very good and Doctor Evil managed to get the price of his meal put on my bill as well. But the receipt the restaurant insisted on giving me was a droll message, handwritten on a scrap of paper: 'Accept for six dollars'.

Word soon spread that there was a stranger in town and along came a gem dealer, who sat down at my table and produced some really lovely jewellery from a battered attaché case. The gold was very yellow and was probably almost pure, but this colour is not attractive to Western tastes. The ruby and sapphire stones were set in marvellous designs, but the prices were too high to take a punt on.

Doctor Evil and I returned to Battembang after picking up another soldier as armed escort. This time, against my better judgement, I was persuaded to sit in the front seat. I managed to find the seat belt, which was in pristine condition, and Doctor Evil clearly thought it quaint that I felt the need of it.

I did not enjoy the front seat all that much. I had to ride with my knees jammed up under the dashboard and I prefer not to see death staring me in the face at each bend of the road. Doctor Evil veered the car from one side of the road to the other seeking the least horrible bits, with the result that we were mostly on the wrong side. I was exceedingly glad to get out of that vehicle and, exhausted, fall on my bed at the Royal until dinnertime.

As usual the food on the rooftop was great. I tried the curry and followed it with their mountainously high fruit plate. I talked with the French couple, Sophie and Emile, and some Norwegians. There was also a big mob of Danish people staying at the Royal, but it was very noticeable that few Americans were travelling. Either September 11 had scared them off, or Cambodia was not on their visiting list. I met only two British travellers, a pair of very striking twin girls. This was Friday night and I could hear a terrific hullabaloo going on across the town, which turned out to be the kick-boxing championships.

It was quite late next morning when I went up onto the roof for breakfast. Once there were only a couple of guests left, one of the boys on the staff took his bath in full view of us. I wish I had that much aplomb. Then I was pleased to discover that the sheets did get washed. Kneeling on the tiled floor of the rooftop, the laundress sang as she scrubbed them. I was surprised at the sweetness of her soft, melodious song.

Dara waited for me downstairs as we had arranged. He greeted me enthusiastically and took me to see a relative of his who owned a shop. Then we mounted Dara's moto and went to visit the railway station. If the train is anything like the station, it must be utterly decrepit. The building and its surroundings were in an awful, falling-down state, grotty and revolting. Then it was on to the museum, which was closed. It doesn't, funnily enough, open on weekends. But, in contrast to the railway station, the museum was a lovely wooden Khmer building, with a façade decorated with blue, red and yellow painted fretwork, peaks and gables. Several attendants sat around a table under the wide veranda playing dominoes and they offered to walk me around inside.

Next we went looking for a pharmacy. I had woken that morning with a funny throat and wanted to buy something to prevent it getting worse. The chemist shop was a hole in the wall with its entire front open to the street; the goods skulked in more holes in the interior walls. For two dollars I bought a tin of Strepsils – you don't see them in tins in Australia anymore, and they are more than twice the price I paid here. Then the girl assistant and I tried to undo the tin. Dara and her helper joined in. We manhandled that tin with all the implements the pharmacy had to offer until, after much effort, we managed to get inside it. To celebrate we each ate a Strepsil.

The hotel manager had told me that there was a minibus going to Phnom Penh the next day and he suggested that it would be better for me to take this rather than the usual share taxi. He arranged for the bus to collect me at the hotel and I got up at half past five, before it was light, in order to cram in some breakfast before leaving. This turned out to be a wise move, as I got nothing else to eat all day. I bid Dara a fond farewell and gave him my old Mazda tennis shade as a souvenir. When I paid the bill for all the food that had accumulated in my room's exercise book, I couldn't believe what it cost. For five days of eating my head off, I paid thirty-two dollars.

The trip to Phnom Penh turned out to be quite a day! By seven o'clock all the passengers were mustered aboard the minibus, which was a twenty-seater in reasonably good condition. There was plenty of room inside, so our luggage was thrown across the back seat and not up on the roof. The other intrepid travellers were a bunch of Cambodians and two spiffy, mature-age French blokes. Really gorgeous guys, they were tall, tanned, sophisticated and so nice there had to be something wrong with them. They had to have handbags hidden in their luggage.

Very soon we were out of Battembang and in the country and moving along quite well, although the road was, once again, appalling and our driver had to bang the bus about and use low gear. I felt sorry for the people we passed who were packed into the back of pick-ups. They were in a full-on dust storm the whole time and even though they had their faces covered with scarves, the rest of their bodies were thickly coated in brown dirt. Roadworks were in progress at places, which made the journey worse, because the detours around them were booby trapped with great holes and their sides were sheer precipices.

The low water-level of the shallow dams that lay in front of each house was evidence of the drought in this part of the country. Some had dried up completely and were mere pans of cracked earth. When we did reach a place where there was a fair amount of roadside water, I was amazed to see hundreds of brown ducks waddling in long rows between the puddles. They looked as though they were migrating, but on foot. Occasionally small herds of cows, attended by a man with a stick, plodded along the side of the road. Beautiful rice paddies extended to the skyline and frequent signs, sky-blue with white writing, advertising the 'Cambodian People's Party' appeared by the roadside.

After two hours travelling, we stopped at a villa-style hotel for what I discovered later, to my extreme sorrow, had been the lunch break. But at nine o'clock in the morning I had presumed it was morning tea and only ordered coffee. We sat down under the veranda of the hotel and I asked the girl who brought the drinks out to us if there was a toilet. At first I was ushered into the kitchen, which was attached to the veranda. The toilet sat dead centre among the cooking in this tin-roofed shed, but before I could proceed into it, another staff member grabbed me, led me up the hotel steps and presented me with a more up-market loo, a real one this time – not a squat job. Maybe she thought I looked too decrepit to make it down to floor level and up again. She wasn't far from wrong either.

We didn't come to much in the way of towns until we got to Champing Char, which was a substantial place. We mostly passed through poor-looking villages, or tiny wayside stalls that consisted of a wooden platform shaded by a thatched roof held up by a few sticks. Each stall was surrounded by a tidal wave of rubbish. This was not the case with the houses, which, no matter how humble, had the living areas around them swept clean. All rubbish was thrown onto the side of the road, or into the dam in front.

We were about halfway to Phnom Penh when the bus's air conditioner broke down. Shortly after that, the engine emitted a loud, consumptive cough and gave up the ghost. The driver opened the lid of the engine, which was inside the bus, and a huge cloud of black smoke poured forth – at which all the passengers scrambled out onto the side of the road.

Two of the Cambodian men went off with bottles and a jerry can, which they filled with water from the ditches beside the road. Then they proceeded to pour this water into the radiator, which didn't seem a very good idea to me. All it did was produce geysers of steam and lots of horrifying noises. I imagine that it might have cracked the engine's head as well. Whatever it did, it did not restore the bus to life. The engine refused to start again and that was that.

Dispossessed, we travellers stood by the deceased body of our former transport under the shade of some large trees. The inhabitants of the nearby house eventually drifted out to inspect us and the lady of the house smiled at me. She had an assortment of children, numbering seven in all, whose sum total of clothing amounted to three pairs of ragged shorts. Their lack of sartorial splendour obviously of no concern to them, the children stood in a line watching us in fascination. Martians would not have got a more detailed study.

One of the Cambodian passengers, a middle-aged woman, showed me that the little plants growing underfoot were sensitive to touch. When you poked a finger at them, they curled their leaves, which resembled small versions of flame tree fronds, into a tight ball.

I was wondering whether the shack of a house we were camped beside had enough beds to put us all up for the night, when I heard a gentle tinkle of bells and from the track alongside the house there emerged two ponderous, plodding water buffalo pulling a cart and wearing the bells that announced their coming. That would be a pleasant way to travel, I thought.

After spending some time beside the road while our bus driver and his helper made numerous calls on their mobile phones, hope of rescue was abandoned and they flagged down a passing utility. It was only a small vehicle and it was already loaded with produce, on top of which perched an abundance of adults and several kids. An arrangement with the utility driver was agreed upon and a rope to tow us procured. We progressed all of a metre before the rope broke and it was back to the drawing board. Someone produced a hatchet, cut down a long, skinny tree about ten centimetres in diameter and setting upon it with the hatchet, chopping wedges out of each end on which to tie the rope. Then the rope was used to secure the tree trunk under the suspension of both the bus and the utility.

Off we moved again. This time we were awfully close together, but we did have a stout pole between us. The effort to drag us along caused the poor utility to belch vast clouds of black diesel smoke which poured in the bus windows as well as the centre-door opening. My seat was in front of this door, but a bar across it prevented me from pitching into the road.

Despite the diesel fumes, the breeze was good. I kicked off my shoes and was waggling my feet in the fresh air when one of the gorgeous Frenchmen said to me, 'You 'ave vairy beautiful feet, Madame.'

I'd much rather he had said face, but beggars can't be choosers, so I made do with the feet.

We travelled very, very slowly, needing many stops. A couple of times the pole came off and had to be re-tied, but at least we were moving in the right direction. Later the sky became exceedingly black and I could see that it was raining up ahead. One of the men and three of the children from the utility crowded into the bus with us. Then we were travelling where heavy rain had fallen recently and the road, bad before when it had been dirt, was now mud and much worse, especially at detours where the mud was churned into deep sticky ruts and there were steep inclines on each side. At one place, ten cars were lined up on the other side waiting for us to manoeuvre our way across. The utility strained and heaved, but it bogged down and became stuck in the mud. A truck came to our aid and with a lot of help from several other drivers, we were eventually hauled free and set off again at our tortoise speed. As we trundled over a wooden-plank bridge I looked down to see big gaps between the boards, which were lifting and falling under our wheels in a most insecure manner.

During our many stops the men relieved themselves, standing by the side of the road with their backs turned. Hours passed and I was getting desperate to do the same, so when I saw the young woman in the group heading for the bushes, I followed her. I waited at a discreet distance until she emerged from behind the shrubbery, then asked, 'Toilet?' She took me by the hand and led me over the mound above the ditch by the side of the road. Making sure that I didn't fall into the plentiful mud, she guided me to a place where I could be half hidden. I was trying to scramble back out of the ditch when she returned to haul me out again.

Another time, when we had stopped so that the men could hack up a replacement piece of wood, I decided that this was a case of now or never. I was high-tailing it across the wilderness when I had a sudden recollection of the guidebook – 'Do not under any circumstances head off into the scrub where there is not a well-beaten path'. Mines! my brain screamed at me. Not to mention little green snakes. I stopped dead in my tracks. There was no beaten path here; there was no path at all. Oh dear. It is well known that the Khmer Rouge mined the rice paddies in order to kill peasants and upset the stability of life. There were no trees or bushes anywhere around, but I stopped right there. My maidenly modestly went out the window when it had to compete with death. I figured that as I always look the other way when the blokes go, they would surely do the same for me, but as I hauled up my trousers I saw one of the dazzling Frenchman staring straight at me across the minefield.

We continued on, even more slowly now and for a very long time. This alleged six-hour bus ride eventually became twelve. Then, hooting and tooting, the cavalry arrived to save the day! A Toyota troop carrier, obviously summoned by our driver, came up behind us. We passengers were de-camped into the Toyota, leaving the bus and the driver still being towed.

In the Toyota the two Cambodian women in our group insisted on sitting next to me. They were definitely not sitting beside one of those great big foreign fellows. I had noticed this before. It's not that Cambodian women were so eager to sit next to me, but they found me infinitely preferable to a male foreigner.

Our new vehicle took off like a comet and very shortly we were travelling on a strip of bitumen that was narrow, but allowed even more speed. From then on the road ran through villages all the way to Phnom Penh, an hour later. Part of the way was through the Muslim village where I saw a couple of mosques and women with their hair covered by scarves or crocheted caps, but not wearing purdah. The larger mosque, I learned, had been used by the Khmer Rouge as a pigsty during its reign of terror, but had been reconsecrated in 1979.

Now, on one side of the road was the river and on the other, behind the villages, water lay on the ground like a swamp. This continued until I recognised the landing from where I had taken the boat to Siem Reap and I realised that we had finally made it to Phnom Penh.

It was dusk when our latest conveyance stopped, but not at the hotel the Royal's manager had intended me to end up at. The only room this hotel had to offer was a horrible hole reached by a set of narrow, grotty stairs attached to the exterior of the building. At the top of the stairs, the person showing me around had to unlock a grille to access the corridor. The metal grille slid back with a clang like those you hear in the best prison movies. We stepped into the really foul little corridor and my keeper opened a door at the end to disclose the room on offer – a tiny windowless cell. Yikes.

With indecent haste I retreated back down the stairs, found a moto and pointed to the river. I knew the Indochina Hotel was somewhere near. Mr Tay, the manager of this now very desirable establishment, greeted me like the prodigal returning, saying, 'Ah, you come back, you come back.'

This time I was given a different room, but the layout was the same. The same carved birds roosted on top of a wardrobe with its full-length mirror that you couldn't see yourself in unless you were on the bed. I began to wonder about these rooms at the Indochina with those mirrors. This room even had a wall light with a red bulb in a glittery, plastic shade. Was I in a brothel, or is this simply the Cambodian idea of what travellers like?

The next day was excessively hot. The temperature reached forty degrees and the humidity was ninety-nine. I am accustomed to the climate of Darwin where the humidity can also reach ninety-nine, but when it does that there, the temperature is usually no more than thirty-four. In this climate I could only be active in the early mornings and evenings, so I goofed off all afternoon and went out later. Walking around the small streets behind the riverfront, I came across a processing shop, left a film to be developed, then asked the assistant, who had a little English, to help me explain to a moto driver that I wanted to go to the supermarket that I had heard was on this side of town. The rider and I eventually found it; a large shop stacked with many local and imported items. I resisted the lure of a goodie labelled 'ultra violent sunscreen', but bought some hair colour. I was in the mood for change. The outside of the box bore the promise that this product would give me 'Beautiful Toes'. I hoped that was meant to be tones. I already had beautiful toes, if I could believe the Frenchman.

It was late, and very dark, when I found a moto driver and asked him to return me to the Indochina. He said he knew where it was, but after a while I realised that we were going in the opposite direction. We stopped so that I could show the rider my map. 'River. Royal palace,' I pointed out to him.

'Oh yes,' he said and took me to the Royal hotel over on the other side of town. When I wouldn't co-operate, refusing to get off his bike and disappear into the Royal Hotel, he took me to the Palace Hotel on the opposite side of town. By this time it was raining. Fortunately I had brought my despised, but useful, hat that kept my hair from looking like a fright wig when I dismounted from motos, and now it redeemed itself even further by keeping me a little dry. Halfway across the city for the third time, now in dark back alleys, I paused to wonder what I was doing. It was pitch black and I was jaunting around in the rain, with no idea where I was, on the back of a moto with someone I didn't know – all things I had been warned repeatedly not to do.

My driver asked several other riders for directions as we rode alongside them and once more we stopped and pored over the map before setting off in another direction. Then I saw the royal palace. 'Royal palace!' I shouted.

'Oh yes,' he said, the penny finally dropping, 'loyal paras,' and from there it was a breeze.

No longer lost, food was next on the agenda. I ate at the Rendezvous Café, a French establishment two doors from the Indochina, on a corner of the promenade. The proprietor was a Frenchman. Far from the bonza sort that had been on my bus from Battembang, he was what I had always imagined French-men in the tropics would be like: middle-aged, paunchy, wrin-kled and worn-looking, but still gallant and attentive.

Restaurants line the footpath all along the riverfront, separated only by rows of pot plants that form green screens. Looking up from my plate I saw a girl of about ten lurking among the plants watching people eat. A tiny naked baby clung to her back as she stood there looking wistful. I gave her my allocation of beggar money for the day. Then a shoeshine boy of about the same age came up to me. Around his neck hung a sign that said, 'I am a deaf mute.' Another young boy came to my table selling the small wreaths of fragrant jasmine flowers that are meant to be placed on altars. I suddenly felt very rich and started throwing money around like a drunken sailor. Blow the guidebooks and their: 'Don't encourage beggars.' These people really need help. But no more money was going to pass from me to monks. The people look after them.

In the morning I woke feeling as though I had been buried or had slept in a cave. I do not like not having a window.

Breakfast at the café on the corner was pleasant, although it was still not really cool despite the breeze that blew in from all sides. Emile and Sophie, the French pair I had met in Battembang, joined me and told me about a great guesthouse out on the lake. I resolved to go there for lunch.

While I was still eating breakfast, I was already planning my next meal. The food along this tourist stretch of the riverfront was, apart from breakfast, no better than it had been in Battembang. I hired a paper and read about the severity of the drought. Five hundred farmers had now come from their villages to camp outside the royal palace.

The moto I commissioned to go to the lake mistakenly took me first to another place on the river. It's all water I suppose. But we made it to the lake on the second attempt. As soon as I dismounted from the moto, I was offered a bag of marijuana. That hurdle over, I loved the place. To reach our destination, the moto and I had jolted down an atrocious rutted dirt lane at the end of which the guesthouse stood with its feet in the waters of the lake. Looking down as I walked along the duckboards that, supported by poles, surround the rooms, I could see the green water between the cracks. The dining and recreational areas were at the end of the guesthouse and poked out into the lake. Here cane chairs and tables, wooden couches covered in cushions and metal swinging seats were bordered by forests of pot plants, orchids hanging in pots from overhead crossbeams and hammocks swinging in the breeze between posts. And the whole place was overlaid with the pungent aroma of ganga.

Not long after I arrived, light rain began drifting down and the breeze off the water was cool. This place was bliss after the baking streets of the city. I ordered a Cambodian dish for lunch. It came with a big fried egg roosting on top of it and was very tasty.

When I climbed onto a moto to return, the rider said that he knew where the Indochina was because he worked at a restaurant up the street. It was only after we were underway that I realised he smelled very strongly of beer. Nice, I thought, now I am out here in all this bedlam with a drunk driver. As I rode around on motos in the crazy Phnom Penh traffic I would occasionally tell myself that I must be mad. But then I would also tell myself that I had survived the roads of South America and that was no mean feat. If I could live through that, I could survive anything. This beer-soaked rider flew happily along, but each time he screamed around a corner at breakneck speed, my feet flew off the pedals. I had learned that the trick to riding pillion is to push down on the pedals like you do in the stirrups to hold yourself on a horse, but we were going so fast on bumpy lanes and streets that this time it was dreadfully hard to do.

Next morning I took a cyclo to the bus station to book a ticket to Sihanoukville, Cambodia's only port on the south coast. I preferred cyclos, but found motos easier to deal with because their riders are mostly younger and sometimes speak some English. Instead of the bus office, this rider took me to the departure point for pick-ups. I counted twenty-one people packed in the back of one of these small utilities and wondered what their life expectancy was – vehicles and passengers.

At ten the following day I went, as arranged, to collect my film. The prints I was given were not mine, but a charming gent kept pushing them back at me with a dazzling smile. He seemed to be saying, 'Just try. I'm sure you'll get to like them.'

The pictures were of a group of Cambodians, none of whom I had ever seen before, in various poses. Finally I convinced the shop assistant that, although I was sure that these were lovely people, I only wanted *my* pictures. He capitulated. With an even bigger smile he said, 'Okay, eleven o'clock.'

I should have known that ten would mean eleven and if I had wanted them for ten, I should have said nine. No one expects you to arrive on time. At eleven I got my pictures without further demur. Then I walked about killing time until my bus left for Sihanoukville. I came upon a local market and was looking at some of the goods when a middle-aged woman patted the tiled platform on which she sat, inviting me to join her. She spoke English and we had a chat in which she told me that if I went to the south coast I should go to see Kampot and Kep, other towns on the south coast.

At the bus station, a row of blue plastic chairs was provided for waiting passengers. I sat down on one and an American girl came and sat next to me. We swapped guesthouse stories until a pedlar decided that he was going to sell me a Zippo cigarette lighter. A fake one. He was as persistent as a sticky fly. Even though he was shooed away three times by the bus station attendant, he kept coming back until he was finally routed by a security guard.

The road to Sihanoukville had recently been improved. The journey took four and a half hours, with a stop at the halfway mark for a feed. The food was lined up in big, lidded aluminium pots on a trestle, where it been sitting all day, cooling down, as much as it ever cools in these temperatures, and busily making bugs. I wasn't all that hungry so I bought a few bananas.

It had been raining down here in the south. Often the rice paddies had water in them, and the small roadside dams were sometimes almost completely covered with huge, brilliant green lotus leaves, as well as the gorgeous pink flowers that were as big as dinner plates.

Plains fan out from the centre of Cambodia and they rise gradually to become densely forested mountain ranges in the south-west and north-east. Closer to the coast I saw open spaces, like raw wounds, where the trees had been stripped and nothing grew except bushes and grass. Then we came to hills that became ever higher as we progressed, until we were passing among heavily wooded, lusciously green hills that rose on both sides of the road. Near the coast I saw roadside spirit houses for Ya Mao, the deity who oversees the south coast.

On arrival at Sihanoukville the bus meandered around the town dropping passengers off at their doors. I waited until the bus came to a permanent stop in the main street and was kidnapped by a waiting moto rider as soon as I stepped down into the dusty road.

7 Encounters of the Spooky Kind

After 1954, when control of the Mekong delta reverted to Vietnam, Cambodia had no sea port, so Sihanoukville was founded in 1959. It is a no-frills country town strung along one wide main street. Situated on a small peninsula that juts out into the Gulf of Thailand, it began life as housing for the port construction workers. Few Western tourists come here; most visitors are Cambodians from Phnom Penh on weekend jaunts. Several fine beaches, separated by rocky outcrops, surround the peninsula and they are the area's main attraction. On them, in anticipation of a deluge of tourists, numerous hotels and guesthouses were built. The tourists never came. Riots in 1997 and 1998 and a toxic waste dump scandal, in which several dock workers died, proved major disincentives.

I showed my moto driver the name of the hotel I had written down. He assured me that I didn't want that one. I thought he was offering to take me somewhere better, so I went along for the ride, which was just what it turned out to be. The accommodation is near the beaches which are a fair distance from the town, so you need a moto to get about. This lad drove me out to Ochheuteal Beach, completely in the opposite direction to Victory Beach where I had decided to go. But Ochheuteal was apparently where my rider thought I should be.

We doddled along the shore, passing hotel after hotel, until I realised that he was waiting for me to 'pick a box'. Cruising to the end of the seafront road, we turned into the street behind the beach and I saw a row of pleasant looking, villa-style guesthouses. I went in to inspect one, another Aspara. All the rooms I was shown had windows, which was good, but they all opened into public space. One stared straight at the washing line that ran under the window in a metre-wide enclosure. Deciding that this area would see a lot of action, I settled on a room that was sparsely furnished, but clean and cool. It was situated in the guesthouse's back quarters with the servants, but its window looked out onto a big stone wall and no one could look in at me.

By then it was a quarter to six and I was looking for nourishment. I'd had nothing to eat all day except two bananas. Leaving my room I noticed two electric plugs that had been installed in the outside wall. They were manufactured only for interior use so half a plastic bucket had been wired above them to shield them from the rain. This looked like a Dodgy Brothers construction job to me.

I walked around to the sea front and came to one of the two up-market hotels, the attractive Seaview. It was shaped like a pagoda with curved and gilded rooftops and had wide verandas and balconies with stone balustrades. It also boasted a garden and a lawn that were fronted by the usual elaborate iron fence, broached by a fancy metal gate that was protected by a guard. Next door was the other posh hotel, the garish, tall, skinny, curved and most peculiar Crystal; the entirety of whose exterior surface, in an effort to live up to its name, some misguided soul had covered with large blue mirror tiles. The effect was startling, to put it mildly.

I went in to the Seaview's lobby for a sticky beak and while I was there I enquired about the prices. The manager showed me a lovely room on the first floor that had big windows with smashing sea views. I was fed up with waking up in a tomb, so the manager and I did some genteel bargaining until the price came down to forty-five dollars, with breakfast. Mr Nygen agreed with me that the first price quoted had been far too much for one person.

The hotel restaurant was downstairs on the sea front. It was open on three sides except for screening rows of plants, from above which pots of orchids with wonderful sprays of cerise, purple, white and mauve flowers hung down. The menu showed surprisingly cheap prices. Listed in three columns, they were, the waitress explained, for small, medium and large. She assured me that small would be 'enough for you'. I was sceptical, thinking, you don't know me, darling. This delicate frame can pack in enough food for a wharf labourer, and twice as fast. But she was right – and before I could order fruit salad to follow, I was presented with a complimentary one.

I was walking back to my guesthouse when I realised that I was again performing a no no. The dark was absolute, there were no streetlights and I was toddling along a beachfront. There was no sign of life, except for the odd moto that whizzed by. I thought of all the times I had been told not to walk around at night. Then, turning the corner, I was in a dirt lane sprinkled with mud and puddles and it was even darker. I felt now that there was more chance I'd break my leg falling in a ditch, than there was of getting mugged.

A lad on a moto came up behind me and rode slowly alongside me practising his English. I think he had been sent by my guesthouse to retrieve me. Just as well, as by then I was, of course, lost. The villas had no signs or lights and now they all looked the same. Finally my escort said, 'Guesthouse Aspara here.' He had brought me home.

I awoke next morning to the sound of birds twittering outside my window. Here on the coast the weather was much cooler and I had not needed the fan on during the night – but I could have done without the cold shower in the morning.

Over the wall that guarded my window I could see a building that looked uninhabited. Last evening I had listened with pleasure to the singing that had emanated from there: several deep male voices raised in harmonious songs that sounded like hymns. At breakfast on the first floor balcony of the guesthouse, I met the only Australian I came across on this trip – a young man called Tony.

'Where are you from?' I asked.

'South Australia,' he replied, 'Adelaide.'

'Me too.'

'Beulah Park,' he added.

'I just sold my flats there,' I said.

Then to my complete astonishment Tony said, 'Yes, I know them. The corner of Thornbury Street.'

Wow! He had lived two doors down from my property for ten years and used to wave to me when I was cleaning up the garden.

Breakfasting among the palms and flame trees that hung over the balcony was divine. From across the road came the shouts and laughter of a group of boys playing soccer and the housemaid was singing underneath the veranda. The guesthouse's pet dog, a petite, fluffy white creature, wandered around the courtyard and a large, fierce-looking Alsatian guard dog, now off duty after his night's work, slept in a wire-netting pen alongside the front gate.

The barefoot waitress brought my food, padding silently on the tiled floor. I was embarrassed then that I had come through the house with my shoes on, uncouth clod that I am. The breakfast was perfect; lots of paw paw, dragon fruit, bananas and pineapple, an omelette and a baguette. There was even the first dish of butter that I had seen in Cambodia. To top it off, there was a big glass mug of the superb coffee.

Once I saw a foreigner foolishly order 'English' tea. He received, for his sin, a glass of lukewarm fluid in which a Lipton teabag skulked, not even colouring the water. It had probably been used before. Local tea is free and, in all places except those catering to Western tourists, a china teapot and glass are plonked on the table as soon as you sit down. The spoggies hung around waiting for the crumbs from my baguette and followed me about like a swarm of flies after a swaggie.

Hearing voices below I peered over the balcony and there were Emile and Sophie again. Before I could yahoo to them they jumped onto a motorbike and roared off. They had said that they were going to rent one and drive themselves around. Brave souls.

Even though I was now moving to an opposition hostelry, the people at the Aspara were happy to help me – maybe they were glad to see me go. They located a moto and negotiated a price that included a couple of hours sightseeing after the driver had deposited me at the Seaview. The rider was the boy who had brought me there the day before. He seemed to have staked some sort of claim on me.

I dropped my bag at the Seaview and signed in. I had booked a single room, but the girl at the desk asked me if I wanted one bed or two.

'I only want one,' I said.

'But two beds is the same price,' she said, and literally forced them on me. It was like, 'you may as well have them if you are paying and you never know your luck, you might find someone to use the other'. So, for a quiet life, I agreed to have two beds.

I put on my hat and we rode off to check out the town and the beaches. It took a while, as the beaches are a fair distance from each other and the town. The coastal area is really beautiful, but the town was dreary. On top of the hill above the town you come to a crossroads and a large roundabout, in the middle of which are two gigantic, gold-painted statues of lions, a male standing and a female crouching. They looked very Disney-cartoonish to me, but the locals are inordinately proud of them.

Past the town, on the side opposite to Ochheuteal, we came to Independence Beach and the seven-storey decaying hulk of the Independence Hotel. Abandoned since 1975, it is said to be haunted. The next beach on from there is Victory, to which backpackers usually gravitate. Between the beaches, the moto and I bumped along small roads and country lanes, whizzing from side to side to dodge cows, pigs, chooks and enormous craters. Just as I was pondering the thought that you were meant to ride motorbikes in an upright manner, not horizontally with the road, Yann, my driver, casually mentioned that he'd hit a cow a year ago. So that was why his face was badly scarred and his mouth a little deformed, I thought. Poor boy. Before this I had never considered the damage an accident on a small motorbike could do to you. Now I wondered about it all the time.

Sihanoukville port is a little further on from Victory Beach and here container ships, and small cargo boats from all over Asia – Thailand, Vietnam, Japan, and Taiwan – lined the wharves, jostling shoulder to shoulder. I read that the Thais have set up extensive shrimp farms along the coast here and not only does ninety per cent of the money go back to Thailand, but the farms are destroying the mangroves.

Back in town I paid off Yann and went into the wonderfully cool little bank. Changing a traveller's cheque was a lengthy procedure, but fortunately a chair was provided. Then I remembered that I should have brought my passport for this operation, but the female cashier said that the photocopy I carried would do. Mind you, the photocopy, the signature and my person came in for some intense scrutiny. I was eventually handed the cash, but you wouldn't want to be in a hurry. The fee for giving me my own money was four dollars for each hundred.

When I entered the bank I had noticed a security guard stationed outside. Shaded by a big striped umbrella, he was comfortably arranged in a plastic chair beside a small tin table. As I came out he stood up and wrote something in a book. I presume it was a comment along the lines of: Peculiar looking foreign woman with pink umbrella and funny hat exits, appears not to have robbed bank, does not seem to have done anything malicious, despite her appearance.

I walked around the streets of the town for a while. There were no beggars and no one hassled me, except the moto riders, who thought that I had no right to be walking. There is only one main street, so I had soon seen it all, including a big roadside sign:

Tyre shop – selling – Mendy Wheels
Reflat
And Fixty.

I spied a big red cross on the outside of one place and decided that this might indicate that it was a surgery of sorts, even though its entire front was open to the street. I stopped for a look and when asked what I wanted, said that I would like my blood pressure taken. A wooden counter fronted the street and behind it a fabric screen partially obscured a patient lying on a trestle bed. The woman doctor insisted on lying me down on the other bed and proceeded to give me the full treatment. I guess she had to make it worth the dollar she charged me. She took my pressure three times with an old-fashioned wooden sphygmomanometer and told me that I measured 13 over 80. I wasn't too thrilled with that diagnosis. At that rate I should be have been long dead. I wrote down '130 over 80?' She agreed. Instantly I felt better.

I bought a supply of bananas and bottles of water and rode back to the Seaview Hotel for siesta.

Goodness me, I was now living in the lap of luxury, wallowing in it in fact. I even had a bath, though I did have to climb up two high steps to mount it. I finally worked out that the big, clunky yellow plastic pipe that ran all around the bathroom – from under the hand basin before it disappeared down a hole in the floor – was actually the drain for the hand basin.

After sufficient self-indulgence, in the course of which I managed to totally stuff up the TV, I went out onto the balcony that overlooked the lovely coconut palm-fringed beach only a few metres away to watch the sunset. It was a pretty enough sight, but I decided that these poor deprived tourists who rave about Cambodian sunsets have never seen the sun sink blood-red into the Indian Ocean off Broome in Western Australia, or sizzle into the sea at Fanny Bay in Darwin.

As I watched, an immense black cloud roared in from the Gulf of Thailand, darkening the waters as it came, until it covered the entire sky. The sea turned from a pale green to a dark, dark grey that was almost black. I waited, and the first welcome drops of rain fell. The south coast has a high rainfall and was not suffering the drought that I had seen in other parts of the country. As the lovely rain splattered down, I hoped that Battembang, and Dara's father, were receiving some too.

Later I took a moto over to the Mealy Chandra guesthouse at Victory Beach. It has a superb position, high on the face of a hill above the beach with eagle-eye views of the sea all around. It was not an eagle, however, but a very large peacock that perched on the edge of the balcony rail, preening his fabulous tail feathers. The Mealy Chandra was reputed to organise tours to the nearby national park that I wanted to visit, but they weren't much help. You needed at least five people.

Deciding to test their food, I stayed for dinner. Seafood is the specialty of this southern region and crabs, prawns and fish were supposedly good and cheap. I ordered a dish called 'steamed fish and garlic' and received a massive slab of fish that proved to be a minefield of bones and came completely covered with garlic cloves and spring onions. I must have been a minefield myself after that. I shared my surplus rice with the resident dog and the young manager came to talk to me. He said that I didn't look 'all-Australian' only half. Intrigued, I asked, 'What's the other half?'

'Half Asian,' he said.

I was beginning to wonder if I am part chameleon. No matter where I go, I get mistaken for half a local. Except China that is. Maybe it was because I'd been at the hair dye again.

On the way home it seemed a good idea to check out one of the several swank new casinos dotted around the beaches. At the entrance I had to run the gauntlet of three grim-looking men who were seated at a table sporting a sign that asked patrons to 'Please Leave Weapons Here'. The guards looked in my handbag but let me in anyway. Once past this barrier I was inside, but – I was alone! The deficiency of customers was, however, more than made up for by an excess of staff – three to each gambling table and a total of thirty in the room. And they all watched me. It's no fun being the only person in a casino, followed by a flock of attendants desperate to do something to earn their pay. I tried a couple of machines and lost the ten dollars that I felt obliged to – it would have been unsporting to take money from this place – and beat a hasty retreat.

Back at the hotel, I asked the manager to reset my TV. It took him ages. He said, 'Someone has altered the settings.' I tried to look innocent and said, 'Tut, tut, they must have.'

The next day I tried the beach. I am not really into beaches – sticky, burning sand and salt is not my cup of tea – but the beaches of Sihanoukville are utterly civilised. Reclining in a deck chair under a palm-thatched umbrella, a low wooden table beside me to keep my belongings from the ravages of the sand and fanned by a cool breeze off the water, I decided that this was definitely the life for me.

The sea was a delight to gaze at, light green near its edge and an enchanting jade green further out. The sky was a screaming azure blue except where business-like cumulus clouds were massing on the horizon.

The water became deep very quickly. No walking for miles

to get wet. Grey-green islands dotted the horizon and close by a headland, covered with lush green palms, projected from the shore, which was lined with feathery pine trees.

Much enterprise was being carried on around me. You could rent a tyre tube to float about on the sea, buy a coconut to drink, or select from a colourful array of fruit balanced on the heads of graceful girls in flat reed trays, or swinging in baskets on shoulder poles. The girls were really just delightful children and they all wanted to stop for a chat. One after the other they plonked down into the deck chair next to me, leaned back and kept me company.

Older women brought trays piled high with large, orange cooked prawns. They looked enticing, but I wondered about their bacteria content. Some women had hot coals in the baskets on their shoulder poles and would cook kebabs for you. The sugar cane juicer wheeled his cart along the shore. He turns the handle on the big wooden wheel that is like a ship's steering wheel and the machine spits out the greenish liquid.

A group of Cambodians were indulging in an orgy of photo-taking at the water's edge. One little girl wore pyjamas, another a yellow tulle party dress and two others were in their white knickers. Swimsuits do not appear to be in vogue for kids. I heard a musical voice singing a cheerful song and turning, saw a blind man with a blue stick being led slowly past busking. From under an adjacent umbrella a scrawny, ferret-faced Frenchman – the type I usually attract attention from – tried to chat me up.

Leaving the beach, I passed a row of change rooms: tiny, one-and-a-half metre high cubicles that were constructed of green plastic stapled onto wooden frames. I peeked inside one. It harboured a huge ceramic pot of water, for sluicing off the sand and flushing the cement floor which doubled as a toilet. If these genteel facilities didn't attract you, there was a tap beside the Seaview's gate with a sign that invited you to 'Feat Washing'.

That evening I met a moto rider who bargained me *down*, the little dear! This was when I learned that the real price for a ride into town was one thousand riel. So far I had been lucky to get it for two. As a female tourist I was usually asked for four. So this time I offered two straight away to eliminate the hassle. 'No,' said the Little Dear. 'One!'

I was stunned. And he also rode like a gentleman. The rider I'd had the night before had scared me witless. Now that I had seen the results of a close encounter of the bovine type, I was extra nervous.

So far I had done everything I had been warned not to do in Cambodia. I had walked about at night, been down by the river after dark, ridden nocturnal motos with unknown riders, as well as using cyclos, all of whose riders are reputed to be ex-Khmer Rouge, like those in Saigon are said to be ex-Viet Cong. I certainly did not set out to do any of these deliberately, they just happened. Perhaps I am lucky, or maybe it is true that the good fairies look after fools and innocents.

In the town centre I located the Casablanca Book Exchange Shop, said to have an English owner who could provide information about onward travel. I swapped two books for one and was sent across the road to a café that I was told could arrange transport to the national park, or onwards to Kampot. Still no luck. It was the wrong time of the year. Almost all tourists around now were from Thailand or Vietnam and they were travelling with their own tour buses. There were no other buses. The only option I had for travelling on was to take a share taxi to Kampot.

I ate dinner at the café, a place with Western-type pretensions, and – will I never learn? – ordered a hamburger. It was appalling. I consoled myself with the extra large bucket of beer that was on special at this, the happy hour. Riding home a little later I made the discovery that being on the other side of an alcoholic beverage helped enormously with the road jitters. Me, not the rider, that is.

In the morning, while helping myself liberally to the hotel's great buffet breakfast, I watched the gardening crew at work. Two little ladies swept the garden paths with fan-shaped brushes, while another trimmed the edge of the lawn with a pair of scissors.

Deciding to make my move to Kampot this day, I took a moto to the share taxi depot in the town. Forewarned that there is no bank in Kampot, I went to change some more money, leaving the moto rider outside the bank with my bag. I felt safe enough doing that with the guard checking me in and out. At the taxi station I waited a good while, but no one else came along who wanted to go to Kampot, so, in the end I had to hire the whole taxi and travel alone. It was only one hundred kilometres from Sihanoukville and it didn't cost much.

Too late I realised that the sensible senior I had negotiated the ride with was not going to be my driver. He handed me over to a very young bloke who jumped in the car and took off like it was jet propelled. Now I understood why the older man had said, 'No! No!' when I had attempted to get in the front seat and had pushed me into the back. I was soon almost jolted into the front seat anyway, as Leadfoot almost cleaned up a moto before we had even made it out of the station yard.

Before long I knew that I was at the mercy of a maniac. We stopped for petrol at the end of the road and, as he pulled back into the street without bothering to see if the road was clear, he nearly cleaned up three people on a motorbike. The offended bikers, instead of screaming abuse at him, glared at me in total disapproval.

We hadn't travelled more than three streets before I was certain that I was the prisoner of the speed demon of all time. I began to speculate about my chances of surviving this trip. Five minutes down the road, the air conditioner packed up. I opened the windows and put on my beautiful hat.

The road from Sihanoukville to Phnom Penh is one of

the few decent pieces of road in Cambodia and, unfortunately for me, I now decided, part of the way to Kampot is along this road. As soon as we reached it Leadfoot, The Maniac, went absolutely crazy. There was a considerable amount of traffic on the road, which made it even more alarming. Driving with reckless abandon, he performed death-defying feats until I could handle no more of it. When he attempted to scream over to the wrong side of the road to pass three trucks going up a totally blind hill, I shrieked at him. 'No, don't do that!'

A little later we roared past a red station wagon. The driver of this vehicle was obviously displeased by this; he immediately pulled out and passed us. This signalled a challenge to Leadfoot and now I was an unwilling participant in a grand prix. We were climbing a steep hill, there were two trucks in front of us, the station wagon was trying to pass us again, Leadfoot revved the engine flat out to prevent this, but eventually it succeeded. Then it was our turn to pass. The race continued, neither vehicle was going to give up, until finally we were over on the wrong side of the road again and a large truck was coming at us head on from the other direction. This was when I spat the dummy. 'Slow down or I am getting out,' I screamed.

'Yes, yes, no problem,' Leadfoot said. They were his only words of English and he probably got to use them a lot if he drove many foreigners.

I recalled another piece of advice from my guidebook: 'The only way to cope with share taxi drivers and Cambodian roads is in the back seat with a bottle of Valium'. I think the writer underestimated it. You need to be in the back seat with a vein full of Pentothal or some other general anaesthetic.

I had read that the road to Kampot passes through some very pretty terrain with parts of the heavily wooded national forest in the background. It could have been desert for all I saw. I was too busy watching the road–someone had to.

Either that, or I had my eyes closed in horror. When I did look about, all I could see flashing past was a green blur. The car's speedo was visible from my position in the back seat, but fortunately it was broken, because I think we were doing about two hundred kilometres an hour and I preferred not to know.

Flying along, we slowed for nothing. We thundered through villages at the same speed as we travelled on the open road, scattering bullock carts, pigs, cows, kids and dogs. Then, when I was almost ready for the coronary ward, we turned off the main road and hit a dirt track. I didn't realise that this was a continuation of the road to Kampot and thought, Oh lord, he's cheesed off with me and now he's going to take me into the bush and leave me for dead.

But despite its appearance, this was the real road: a sheet of dirt which, due to the recent rains, had become mud. We went as fast as we could on this, which meant that we slid from one side of the road to the other, as there weren't any potholes to stop us. It was still raining and the windscreen wipers slapped mud everywhere. But now that my driver had been forced to slow down a little, I could see that the countryside was very beautiful; broad expanses of green rice paddy interspersed every now and then by a stand of coconut palms around a house and a line of blue hills on the distant horizon. The half-grown rice looked in good condition. There was a lot of water around – much of it in the car and on me via the window.

Then the road turned into a narrow strip of bitumen between large potholes – not potholes in bitumen, this was bitumen in between potholes. We banged and bashed on this for the rest of the way to Kampot, lurching through villages and fields where boys sat on buffalos, and pushing through a couple of herds of cows that narrowly escaped with their lives and limbs. We clattered and clanged, making an alarming racket, over several bridges, all of which sported big gaps.

Kampot started with a few scattered humble wooden

houses, then a better one popped up every so often until, crossing an impressive bridge over a wide river, I saw the Marco Polo Hotel and the few other imposing French colonial buildings that stand majestically on the river's far bank. This was the only pretty aspect of the town.

My driver had never heard of the guesthouse I requested, so he took me to the bus station in an attempt to get rid of me. After asking directions of many people, one man got in the car and drove us to my destination, where I received the usual joyous welcome. I am sure that it is not just that they want your money. Cambodians are simply very nice people. Except that bloody Leadfoot.

I had come to roost in the Kampot version of the Mealy Chandra Guesthouse, a traveller's haunt, where I met more people in half an hour than I had met in the two days that I stayed at the posh hotel. It is all very well to be comfortable, but you don't meet other travellers. The people who stayed at the Seaview were well-off Cambodians and tour groups from Thailand and France, none of whom spoke enough English for a chat.

Kampot is a provincial capital, a quiet, laid-back place one hundred and forty-eight kilometres from Phnom Penh. Due to the former lack of security in this region, it has not been open to travellers for long and few tourists come here. In the nineties the Khmer Rouge killed six foreigners that they had kidnapped from the road or the train to Sihanoukville.

The Mealy Chandra Guesthouse is on a corner not far from the central roundabout, which is the main hub of the town. One side of it fronts a wide road, but the lane on the other side looks very rural. You enter the guesthouse almost directly off the street, from under a spreading tree that harbours the small wooden spirit house in which the rightful owner of the land and the tree lives. As I passed the spirit house I noted, from the contents of its offering tray, that this spirit was partial to lotus buds.

And where else in the world would you be greeted with the delightful sight of two gorgeous, pink pigs squealing, wallowing and foraging in the wet grass and mud puddles beside the hotel's entrance as you arrived?

My room was on the second – the top – floor and it was massive. It contained two wooden beds and a cane hat stand to put your clothes on. In the Seaview I'd had to keep turning off the air conditioner because it was too cold, but here I had a fan over the bed which was much more comfortable.

From the wide balcony outside, I looked down to see a mass of purple bougainvillea scrambling over the roof. Coconut trees and small palms interspersed with orchids framed the sides of the building and at the rear, separated by a rough paling fence, the rice paddies began.

The extra bed for emergency guest accommodation was kept in the corridor outside my room. A huge apparatus and a real bush carpenter job, it was covered with a bright red sheet and had four high wooden corner posts, from which hung a blue mosquito net. This was where those travellers who came late and found the place full were put up.

Another emergency bed was kept in an alcove under the stairs on the ground floor, and under it lived a disabled dog. I often saw a girl lovingly feeding this poor creature, whose front legs were paralysed so it couldn't walk. You'd have thought it would have been donged on the head, but it was very well cared for. Now and then during the day, the staff would carry it to the back door so that it could sit in the sun and watch the activity in the yard.

I asked the girl feeding the dog if it was sick. 'Yes,' she said, 'he is sick a long time.'

Fido realised that I was talking about him and he began to shuffle along the tiles in my direction, looking for a pat.

The guesthouse cooking was done in the back yard and the cook lived in situ in the cookhouse. Standing on the balcony I could see down into this little humpy. It had a roof and sides up to waist level, while the rest was open. It was probably very clean, but it looked extremely basic. Following my standard policy of never looking too closely at gastronomical arrangements – not if I intended to keep eating – I averted my eyes.

The Mealy Chandra's household utensil that I coveted was an ingenious device they had constructed for removing cobwebs from their exceptionally high ceilings: a feather duster attached to a bamboo pole that must have been four metres long.

That night I ate dinner in the guesthouse café that doubled as a foyer and a sitting room for the staff and guests. It wasn't the best food, but the staff were a jolly, smiling lot. The waiter pulled up one of the cane chairs and joined me, offering a bite of the thick slice of raw eggplant he was chomping on. Street vendors sell these goodies, apparently regarded as delicacies, stuck onto a sliver of bamboo like a giant lollypop.

I asked for some fly spray to fumigate my room, as it had no insect screens. But at least I had windows, two even! Then, while I was waiting for the air in my room to clear, I watched an awful film on the café's video with the staff and two French blokes.

The pigs were still squealing and oinking up and down the dark street and I wondered to whom they belonged. They, like the free-ranging ducks and chooks, must know where home is when they are ready to retire.

I slept comfortably under the fan after stripping the lone sheet off the other bed to use as a shield against the mozzies. A short while into my slumbers I was shocked awake by a bright light that flashed on at the far end of my room. I was convinced that someone was in the room with me, until I realised that the shiny laminex sheets that had been tacked up to form a flimsy partition between my room and the next, contained a five-centimetre gap that ran from the ceiling to the floor. If I had felt so inclined I could have peered through it to view the inmates next door. I sincerely hoped they hadn't had the same idea when my light had been on. They were making a great deal of noise in there. I don't know what they were doing, but it sounded like fun.

I awoke to grey pelting rain. It was wonderful, cooling and cleaning. At the first glimmer of light the locals started to stir, to the accompaniment of a cacophony of sound from roosters, chooks, ducks and motos. I had a leisurely breakfast in the Mealy Chandra café which, being on a corner, was open on two sides to the street, and where, centre stage, three dogs performed a ménage a trios. Over and over. Then another dog, and another, joined them. I couldn't depart in the pouring rain, so I was trapped there with the boys and girls on the staff, who regarded the spectacle impassively, as though they were at the pictures.

The Buddhist shrine, bedecked with red lights, flowers and offerings of fruit and rice in tiny bowls, held pride of place in a prominent corner of the café. The guesthouse owner came along with a small radio, which he turned on and set down on the floor by the shrine. Maybe the house god needed to hear the news. Above the shrine hung a life-sized, coloured photo of King Sihanouk. In almost every building I entered, I saw a picture of the king, sometimes with his queen. Although the king has only the power of a constitutional monarch, he is popular with his people and is revered by many in the way that the God-kings of old were.

The rain turned the dirt track alongside the guesthouse into a muddy, flowing stream. Earlier I had wondered why the old wooden houses opposite were all on stilts. Now I knew – that side of the street had become a canal. Great for the multiplication of mosquitos. The ducks were going berserk; quacking ecstatically they splashed, waddled and preened, flapping feathers and wings. Geckos and frogs appeared to add to the hubbub. A girl came out of a house across the way and stood collecting the rain run-off from her thatched roof in a yellow plastic basin. Thunder cracked and rumbled and

137

black clouds rolled past. A few brave souls ventured out shrouded in plastic and umbrellas sprouted. Water gurgled into the waiting earthenware jars beside the houses from the downpipes of the roofs.

It rained so hard that water came into my bathroom. I got a shower through the wire netting of the glassless window as I cleaned my teeth at the basin. Looking up, I saw that a bird's nest, part of which dangled untidily into the room, had been built between the wire and the wall. Later I heard tiny cheeps coming from the nest.

Across the street from my room was a private school. It was not in a regular school-type building, but occupied the second and third floors of the kind of structure, rounded on the corner in the Cambodian style, that is used for business offices. From seven in the morning I heard children chanting their lessons. And the poor little beggars only got one day off. Even on Saturdays they had to go to school.

My bathroom had no plug for the hand basin, but a plug the right size for a bath, which I didn't have, sat on it. This had possibly been left there for me to admire. The squirter on the end of the hose beside the toilet, that by now I had realised was standard equipment, did not have the usual nozzle. Instead, the end of it was folded over and secured with a rubber band which, when released a little, did the job. Then you hung it back up on the hook on the wall. I had found this hose to be a very handy gadget for washing my feet, but when I picked this one up for the first time I must have shot the red rubber band off. I saw something land in the water of the toilet bowl and start wriggling. Thinking, Lord! whatever is that? I stared, horrified, at this creature that squirmed and gyrated about in the toilet, until I finally twigged that it was the rubber band. It stayed there. I sure as all get out wasn't fishing it out.

At the Marco Polo Hotel I arranged to do a trip to the Bokor National Park and the abandoned French hill station of

Bokor. High and remote in the mountains, forty-one kilometres from Kampot, Bokor is home to many endangered species. Although poachers threaten tigers, Cambodia has been inaccessible for such a long time that some species which are extinct elsewhere in Asia are thought to still exist here. In various locations in the country there are elephants, leopards, tigers, rare storks, wild ox, Javan rhinos, some of the last remaining Irrawaddy freshwater dolphins, giant catfish up to five metres long, Siamese crocodiles, giant ibis, marbled cats, piloted gibbon, brown antlered deer and horseshoe bats.

At the ungodly hour of seven one morning, the guide, a man named Sim, shunted me into a Toyota four-wheel-drive twin cab utility. We collected a young English couple from another guesthouse, then messed about until after eight looking for the French couple who were supposed to join us. At this hour pigs of all sizes roamed the verges of the town streets and one very large white Brahman bull was tethered under a tree. Finally the muster was completed and Sim drove us to buy baguettes to take with us. This was when I was rudely awakened to the fact that lunch wasn't going to be forthcoming unless I provided it myself. I'd only managed coffee that morning at the Mealy Chandra. The cook had been at the market buying the eggs and bread for breakfast when I left. The bakery we went to was an old, dark stone house, its exterior stacked high with piles of neatly chopped firewood ready for the ovens – the bread produced by which proved excellent.

The young English couple were very nice. They had smashing Oxford accents – under interrogation they admitted that they were both studying at that university. Paul was exceptionally good-looking in a classical way, courtesy of his Indian parentage. Claudia had a horrible metal object stuck through the middle of her bottom lip and pink and purple tiger-striped hair. The French couple were pleasant too, but very ordinary looking after this startling pair.

Off we shot, scattering bikes and barely missing pedestrians. Another lunatic driver! The roads, apart from a couple in the main part of the town, were all narrow dirt and we followed one of these for a while. Very soon we started to climb and then there was no road at all, just a strip of cleared jungle that was all rocks and ditches. Undaunted, Sim drove hell for leather up the steep incline, knocking the poor vehicle about like crazy. The Frenchman, who had opted to stand in the back of the pick-up for a better view, soon was banging on the back window, frantic to come inside. He squeezed into the front seat with Sim and me, which left me with one leg either side of the floor gears. Going up, up, and up was bad enough, but Sim flew with carefree abandon down the mountainsides, the drops over the edge becoming longer and scarier by the minute. At least I couldn't see where the falls over the side ended because, thankfully, the jungle grew so tall and dense all around the path that the sight of our impending doom was obscured.

The road, so-called, was merely a narrow broken track of rocks. Nothing has been done to this path since the French left and only the occasional glimpse of a tiny spot of bitumen among the jumble of red earth and rock gave a clue to the former existence of a decent road. The climb continued forever, through palms, bushes, creepers and trees that sometimes formed a green tunnel so narrow that bamboo and palm fronds smacked the windscreen and bashed the sides of our vehicle as we pushed our way through.

Reaching the gate of the National Park, we had to fork over money, supposedly for park maintenance, but this obviously didn't include the road. Not long after entering the park, we stopped briefly at the humble shrine of the spirit of the mountains so that Sim could say a prayer and make an offering. I noticed that he didn't accord the same respect to the glitzy Buddha statue that stood in an open-sided, gilt roofed pagoda beside the road a little further on. Our next stop was King

Sihanouk's villa. Built on the extreme edge of a precipice, with a tremendous drop beneath, its semi-circular, open-fronted portico gazes out over a lovely panoramic view down the mountains and valleys to the sea. Far away I could see Kampot and further on around the coast, the seaside resort of Kep. Off the coast lay a large island that Sim petulantly said had been Cambodian before the Vietnamese took it away from them. Close by was the king's meeting house, also with a spectacular outlook. But everything was derelict, initially trashed by the Khmer Rouge and then left for the weather to complete the task.

Sim showed us the local killing fields. He said that the Khmer Rouge had brought thousands of people up here to exterminate them. Why they had bothered transporting them up this difficult road beat me, unless it was for the secrecy its isolation gave. The Khmer Rouge would drive truckloads of their victims to the edge of the eighteen hundred metre high precipice that I now stood on and tip them off.

This had been the fate of the Bokor casino's French manager and his wife and children, who had been unable to escape before the Khmer Rouge took Bokor. Many of the Cambodian teachers and other intelligentsia who were brought here for execution, had been told that they were being taken for re-education. Some victims were merely stood on the edge and knocked over.

We travelled on, up and over several more mountains, sixteen in all, Sim said, to finally reach Bokor hill station. Founded in 1922, it stands at one thousand and eighty metres. The eeriest, ghostliest place in the world, Bokor was off-limits to travellers for a long time and has only recently been re-opened. The Khmer Rouge over-ran Bokor in 1972 and remained a menace in the district until lately. Now the dangers a visitor faces come from illegal loggers, poachers and landmines, all of which can cause you serious harm if you get in their way.

The hill station had been built at a great height on a bleak treeless plateau, said to be inhabited by wild elephants, but I saw only their dung. There were no streets, the buildings sat on small sections of flat land, like tiny platforms, looking at each other across little dips and rises, and wherever possible, they had been built on the edge of a precipice looking out at the magnificent view. The French colonists had established Bokor as a refuge from the worst of the heat. It had been a thriving village with a school, a restaurant and a Catholic church that, placed high on one hill, looked across at the marvellous casino-hotel on another. During the 1979 Vietnamese invasion of Cambodia, the Khmer Rouge made the church their headquarters, the Vietnamese took the casino, and from these two points, half a kilometre apart, they lobbed shells and shot at each other for three months.

Both buildings are now in a state of decrepitude, but you can still see what a fabulous place the hotel casino was. It is situated on the outermost edge of a steep mountainside, offering wonderful vistas. From its ground level patio, the balconies of its three floors, and the rooftop and battlements, you look out over mountain slopes and valleys to the sea. Some of its grandeur lingers, the beautiful parquet and tiled floors, marble spiral staircases and columns are still there, but they are steadily succumbing to the inexorable march of time and the intrusion of the wilderness. Mould creeps over the stonework and fingers of greenery explore the possibilities of toeholds in nooks and crannies.

I walked with reverence – there is a powerful feeling that ghosts abide here – up the wide entrance steps and into the great, lofty ceilinged ground floor to stand among the grand marble columns that soar to the roof. Gazing at the massive stone fireplace, I thought how wonderful all this must have been in its day and felt immensely sad to see it so wrecked. It wasn't hard to believe that it is generally thought to be haunted. There was definitely something spooky about this place.

I ascended the marble stairs to the ballroom and the hotel suites and began to descend the narrow spiral staircase that led to the basement kitchens. Halfway down I baulked. Something in me refused to go any further down that little flight of steps. Discussing it later with our group, I found that the others had felt the same.

The park rangers live in one of the few remaining houses. You can stay with them overnight and they will take you for a hike. You can't go alone because the entire area, except for the paths we walked along under the supervision of our guide, is mined. I saw the red and yellow posts that warn of mines sticking up out of the ground at intervals along the sides of the paths. When I asked why the mines had not been cleared, Sim said that some had been, but that it was too hard to get experts up here to do it. He stressed repeatedly that we were only to tread the paths that he told us were okay. I only needed to be told this once. You would have to be completely stupid to wander off on your own here.

Bokor's supernatural atmosphere is enhanced by the fact that it is virtually up among the clouds and that they roll in and out so rapidly. I stood on the edge of the casino patio that hung out over empty space, and watched as cloud poured up like smoke from the valley, obliterating everything as it came. One moment I could see down to the coast and the sea and the next I could see nothing. It had all completely disappeared. One minute I could look across and see the Catholic church with its tall, pointed steeple and the next it was gone and I was alone in a white fog. Then the wind blew and the church emerged from the drifting mist like something out of *Brigadoon*. It was, like in a ghost movie, there one second and gone the next.

Back in the Toyota, we drove a kilometre or so down from Bokor to eat our baguette lunch outside a wat called the Five Rocks Pagoda. Named, not surprisingly, for the five large rocks that it nestles against on the edge of another precipice, it has a magnificent view. The Khmer Rouge blew it up and it is the only thing in these parts that has been re-built. I guess this was what was important to Cambodians. Two ancient monks live in the Five Rocks Pagoda, along with the bones of the king's grandfather and their three-legged dog of the bitsa variety, the now familiar Clayton's Corgi.

Further on down the mountains we stopped so that the other intrepid travellers could take a two-hour hike through the jungle – populated by hordes of leaches and mosquitoes, not to mention wild elephants and tigers – to visit a waterfall. I gave this a big miss. Though I would have liked to see some tigers and elephants, I've seen heaps of waterfalls and mosquitoes. Sim said that there were also wild pigs and deer, but we saw no animals at all. I reclined my seat, made myself comfortable and started reading a book, but I soon fell asleep and had a very nice siesta. I only woke up when Sim's ruddy phone, which I had been given custody of, along with the baggage, rang. I did not answer it. Not only because I can't speak Cambodian as yet, but I also don't know how to answer a mobile phone. I am still only *thinking* about joining the twenty-first century.

By the time we began our descent it had started to rain. On the way up we Nervous Nellies had repeatedly told Sim to drive slowly. Now, coming down in the pelting rain with the de-mister not working and the windscreen obscured so that it was impossible to see where we were going, he finally listened to us and slowed a little. Before long we were driving in a fast-flowing downward stream of muddy water and it was very dangerous. When we rolled down the windows to clear the mist from the windscreen, wet bamboo and bushes slapped in. It took a long while to get back to Kampot, but we eventually arrived safely.

At the Mealy Chandra I found Emile and Sophie sitting in the café. Since I had first met them on the bamboo train in Battembang, they had continued to pop up wherever I went.

In Phnom Penh I stayed next door to them on the riverfront. Then they were in Sihanoukville and now Kampot. Cambodia is a relatively small country and the few travellers who venture further than the temples of Angkor may find that their paths cross more than once. I had intended eating at a restaurant further along the street that was said to have good food, but I couldn't be bothered. After a day on that awful road, I was beat. All I was fit for was to eat in the Mealy Chandra's café.

Kampot shuts down at eight at night anyway. All the lights are out by nine and after that the streets are pitch black. The electric power also went off, sometimes for hours, during the day and if your establishment didn't run to a generator – and the Mealy Chandra didn't – it was pretty hot without the fan. I went to bed early and slept well, apart from the neighbours throwing the light on in my eyes like a searchlight. Towards morning there was the most gosh-almighty storm. Thunder shook the building and it teemed with rain. Nice, I thought, this is the day I have chosen to go for a long ride on a moto. I had made a deal with a rider the previous evening.

The morning was still pretty black, but the rain had stopped. I was the first guest in the café where I found the waiter sweeping the concrete floor with a straw fan broom. But the birds were already up and doing and the ducks, following the rain, had been busy since first light. I watched the wooden horse carts clopping by in the street as I waited an age for my breakfast. It must have been market time again. Then, before I got any tucker, the moto rider arrived.

I had decided to go to Kep, twenty-five kilometres away. Until the 1960s, Kep had been Cambodia's beach resort town. Having weighed the risk of accidents and the damage to my nervous system involved in taking a share taxi, I had settled for a motorbike.

Off we went, very carefully, as I had been promised. We passed through the middle of Kampot's market, which is just around the corner from the guesthouse, and my driver told me that it was busy today because it was Sunday, the big market day. The unmistakable pong of fish hit me, but we soon cleared the market and the town and were out in the country.

The main hazard for moto riders is the possibility that a vehicle will knock you off the bike, but the traffic today was mostly bikes, other motos and bullock or horse carts. The only vehicles that passed us were a couple of mini-vans chock full of people going to picnic on seafood at Kep. One came really close to us and that was when I put my bag between the driver and me. I had visions of its strap getting caught and ripping us both off.

For most of the way the narrow road ran right beside the beach, except for when, now and then, a little village sat on the shore. On the other side the countryside was deliciously green; it rains almost every day along this coast. Rice fields extended to the line of blue-grey hills on the horizon. Some fields were verdant patches of paddy and in others farmers ploughed with oxen and wooden ploughs and women planted the young shoots.

We passed through a fishing village that belongs to the Islamic Cham people, where all the women wore headscarves and long dresses. I was intrigued to learn that Cambodian Muslims call the faithful to prayer by banging on a drum like Buddhists do, rather than with the voice of the muezzin.

About halfway to Kep it started to rain. We stopped and sheltered at a roadside fruit stand. The rider put on his raincoat and I pulled my precious hat down over my eyes and scrunched up behind him for shelter. A little rain doesn't worry me – ironically I had been afraid of sunburn and was covered with buckets of sunscreen.

The first roadside sign we came to on the outskirts of Kep was that of the Seaside guesthouse. It was a welcome sight and I received a warm welcome, even though I arrived dripping wet and paddled in like a duck, squelching puddles all over the clean tiled floor.

Now simply called Kep, Kep-sur-mer was established in

1908 as a seaside retreat for the French elite. Now the Cambodian elite comes here for gambling and water sports, while lesser folk make weekend day trips to picnic on the cheap and plentiful seafood for which it is famous. A few grand villas are dotted around, but most of the place is in ruins. Local people looted whatever they could sell in order to survive the famines of 1979 and 1980.

The Seaside guesthouse is an utterly delightful villa-type building in the world's best position, right on the sand of a beach where the sea washes up to crash against a garden wall shaded by frond-waving coconut palms and Indian almond trees with large, dark-green leaves.

I dried out quickly, but by then the rain was hammering down and I was marooned in my room. At half past eleven the sky brightened a little and I went downstairs to order lunch in the café that was attached to one side of the guesthouse. The menu read:

Fish the Grilled
Fish on Hot Oil
Fish the Distil
Brawn the Grill.

I ordered prawns and received a huge plate of smallish affairs. It was an Herculean task to peel them all and they didn't come with a finger bowl, although I did get a roll of toilet paper disguised as serviettes. The dipping sauce was divine and I mopped up the leftover amount with a couple of baguettes. I know it is bad manners to dunk bread in your gravy, but it was too good to waste.

The girl who brought my food from the kitchen had a really terrible graze, painted bright yellow with Betadine, all down one side of her face. I asked her how she got it and ruefully she said, 'Moto bike.' And here I was thinking I'd done the smart thing in giving the share taxi a miss.

It was pouring again by the time I had finished lunch, but I loved it at the Seaview. I could hear the sea in my first-floor room. And if I sat on the balcony outside, I could admire it. The balcony looked straight out to sea, interrupted only by a line of thatched roof gazebos down by the garden wall. Today the wide expanse of ocean was grey, angry and covered with white caps. Waves pounded on the wall only a few metres from my balcony. Despite the wind and the rain one hardy guest reclined, reading, in one of the hammocks that were secured between the poles of the sheltering gazebos.

My bathroom came with the regulation-issue comb and tooth mug. I never used either. This comb was bright red and appeared to have been well patronised. Although I had seen toilet paper holders in some pretty inconvenient places, this one took the cake. It was on the wall at the opposite end of the room, chest high between the basin and the vanity mirror. I came to the conclusion that they don't do these peculiar things with the toilet paper out of devilment, or to make life difficult for you. I think it is simply that they are not terribly sure what its actual use is. But I am always so grateful to be given any at all, that I don't care where they put it.

It continued raining after lunch and I continued sitting on the balcony. There was no electricity during the day – the generator did not roar into life until six-thirty in the evening – and even with a big window with a spectacular sea view, it was too dark inside my room. The cool breeze was great, but I soon had to retreat into the doorway as a heavy misting of rain swept in across the sea and blew over me. I retreated further as it intensified. Then everything was obliterated. The sea and sky were gone and little rivers now ran down through the guesthouse grounds to meet the sea.

After a couple of hours the weather finally cleared and I began sloshing through the mud of the track that led from the Seaview to the road. I was surrounded by so much green that it was almost too much, layer on layer, shade on shade of it, brightened now and then by a splash of colour – red, purple and white flowers on bushes and the mauve and lilac blossoms of rain trees, which had no excuse not to be flowering. Fat, roly-poly pink piglets, tails wiggling in ecstasy, grubbed busily among the roadside plants. Sometimes the only visible part of them was a corkscrew tail waving from the bushes. Pigs are always so busy. They are never indolent unless they are having a well-earned lie down in the mud – they use mud as a sunscreen to protect their tender skins.

The road, when I reached it, was a winding strip of black asphalt that curved up and around gentle rolling slopes. I walked along it slowly. There was no wind, no sound at all. It was so peaceful and bucolic it took my breath away. More pigs rooted around in the grass, chooks scratched and flapped and a herd of tan cows, with two tiny poddies at their heels, quietly munched grass. Although there was much fodder for the cows, they were still only in fair shape, but the buffalo were fat and glossy. Dodging the cow flaps on the road, now and then I passed a thatched, wooden-framed house with plaited reed walls. Children swam in the ponds in front of the houses.

In places the road, which ran parallel to the coast, was completely covered overhead by all-embracing flame trees. On the inland side the land inclined sharply away to become steep hills covered with dense green forest that looked uninhabited. I came to a magic spot. Like a jewel in a beautiful setting, a big pond covered with pink lotus blooms lay surrounded by small, lush green palms, while larger palms banked up in tiers behind them on the rising ground.

Further and further, passed only by a couple of motorbikes, I hiked along this lonely road. Then a car whizzed past me and came to a screeching halt. Both its front doors flew open and two men leapt out. Kidnapping and mugging! my mind shrieked. But one man dashed off to one side of the road and the cover of a convenient bush, while his companion raced to the other side and ran along looking for similar means of concealment. Up-market blokes these. By the time I had drawn level to the man nearest me, he was still looking for camouflage and hadn't managed to get out of my range of view. I put my hand over my eyes and said, 'It's okay.' He roared with laughter, flashing me a wonderful display of his gorgeous gold teeth.

I seemed to walk forever before I came to a small roundabout that was overshadowed by an enormous poster containing a series of pictures that depicted women massaging men. It looked like an advertisement for pornographic behaviour. Was it a school for scandal? A house of ill repute?

Skirting the roundabout I came to the seashore. Here, as evidenced by piles of prawn and crab shells, was where the seafront picnics were held. But I had come too late. The seafood pig-out was over. No one remained except a lone vendor sitting cross-legged among the wreckage of the feast.

Still, the beach was exactly how I like a beach to be. A footpath shaded by big trees meandered beside a low wall, on the other side of which waves washed on the shore only a metre of golden sand away. On the land side of the narrow road, sets of steps climbed the hillsides to rough bough shelters with log seats, where you could picnic with an elevated sea view. Picking my way among the crab and prawn shells that lay everywhere, I ambled along the path beside the sea wall and came upon two men who were tying up the power lines in preparation for cutting back a tree. I presumed the wires weren't live, but held my breath anyway.

Further on, the hill on the land side rose even more steeply and on it, now and then, perched a villa looking straight into the sea. What is left of Kep is sprinkled along this small headland.

I began searching the landscape for a moto to give me a ride back to the Seaview, but I walked kilometres and saw none, and was nearly to Vietnam before one finally came along. I hopped on the back – but not for long. After about a kilometre we conked out. The rider gave the bike a good shaking, then gave up. I started to walk again, I hoped in the direction of some kind of civilisation. Soon I saw a wonderful sight, a petrol station. I thought that I'd buy a bottle of juice and return to the moto, but this place only had pumps. Then I saw the moto rider pushing his bike towards me. I bought the bike some petrol – the poor lad had no money, of course – and we agreed, or so I thought, that he would take me back to my guesthouse.

We had ridden a long way down the road before I realised that we still seemed to be heading towards Vietnam. I called a halt and turned the bike around. I think the rider had been waiting for me to recognise the place I wanted.

By the time the generator finally came on, it was already pitch black in my room and the light was gratefully received. The restaurant had two-candle-power lighting. I sat directly under one lamp and I still couldn't see a thing, not even the food. I had ordered fish and could tell that this was what I got only because the object on my plate was fish shaped, complete with a tail. It filled the large plate, but when I tried to cut it, I found nothing except bones and skin. It was quite inedible. I gave up the effort of trying to cut it as a bad job and asked for some rice and vegetables. Settling my bill in the morning I saw that I had not been charged for the fish. They hadn't taken offence at my rejection of their food. Perhaps they were used to it. I felt mean about this though, so I gave them some extra money. Once again I was struck with the generosity of the Cambodian character.

8 Lady of the Lake

No food was forthcoming from the Seaside's kitchen early in the morning, so I set off up the road looking for the small restaurant that I had heard about from a fellow traveller in the café last night. Taking the first turn left, which I now know should have been the second right, I began climbing a precipitous hill. It became steeper and steeper until, gasping and groaning, I reached the top. There I saw a sign saying 'Vella Guesthouse'. I had heard that this was an enchanting place to stay, but I would never have found it except by a happy accident such as this. Guests were accommodated in tiny, thatched Khmer-style bungalows that had been built into the side of the hill and had a spectacular view out to sea.

Nearby, among the lush green jungle, I found the guesthouse's minute café and here a beaming young woman produced a marvellous onion omelette for me. I had learned not to order cheese, but Cambodia has onions a-plenty. I love onions and my omelette was stuffed full of them, cooked to golden perfection.

The café was merely a wooden platform, open on three sides, which clung to the hillside supported by poles made from tree trunks. A low, plaited cane balustrade formed a barrier between the patrons and the precipice, while a line of clay pots containing orchids in flower hung down to frame the view from the edge of the palm-thatch roof. The kitchen was a woven rattan lean-to at the rear, in which I could see the cook washing dishes on a bamboo floor. Her small girl sat crooning happily to herself, naked and cross-legged, on the floor in a corner.

Only the occasional sound of a moto drifted up from the road far away below and, looking down over the green hillside, through which the red roofs of a couple of villas peeped, I could see all the way to the sea with its islands and boats.

I walked back down the mountain and, deciding that it looked as though it was about to rain all day again, I opted to return to Kampot. Rain is great, but it does limit sightseeing after a while. During the night I had been woken several times by stupendous thunderstorms, great rolling claps of thunder that went on for ages accompanied by torrential rain. Between storms I could hear the soothing sound of the sea flinging itself against the garden wall only a few metres away.

I commissioned a moto for the return ride, on the condition that the rider would proceed with great care. He agreed with the usual brilliant smile. We had not ridden far toward the black cloud ahead of us when he stopped and, saying something like 'I get somebody', dashed into a wooden hut by the side of the road. Lovely, I thought, now we are going to be three on this bike – but he returned with one of the canary yellow plastic rain capes that moto riders wear and proceeded to dress me in it.

We trundled on and halfway to Kampot the rain started. I had been watching the thunderous black cloud slipping away to the hills and thought that it might bypass us. But Murphy had other plans and the next minute we rode smack into it. The rider stopped and swaddled me tighter into my yellow cocoon. I was wearing my hat and big sunglasses, but my legs became soaked. The further we continued, the heavier the deluge became. From my close-up vantage point behind my driver, I watched large raindrops form on the lobes of his ears and hang there, like glittering crystal earrings, until they fell off and others began to take shape.

By this time we were in open country and there was

nowhere to stop. My driver wanted to push on and get it over with, so I agreed. I couldn't get much wetter.

As soon as we stopped at the Mealy Chandra and I stepped off the bike into the warm air, I began to emit clouds of steam. The staff thought it was a huge joke that I was such a mess. My feet and legs were covered with mud from the puddles we had splashed through and the bridges we had banged over, there were little deposits of grit all over my face and the creases of my eyelids contained compost heaps. I tottered into the café, doing a good impression of a drowned rat. Sodden hat streaming onto my shoulders, face running with water, not to mention dirt, I squelched up the stairs. But I had been welcomed back like a long-lost relation and was given the best front room again.

After I had mopped myself, I went to the market, jumping over and sloshing through puddles to get there. Although this road was one of Kampot's best, it was still a dodge-the-potholes and slip-and-slide-in-the-mud affair.

I had a wonderful time in the sprawling market. No one hassled me and I didn't have to bargain. The prices I was charged were pretty much the going rate – I think. Whatever – it was cheaper than Phnom Penh. For eight dollars I managed to buy a huge assortment of goods – mirror, tapes, comb and a family sized (the only one available) tin of fly spray that, according to its label, would keep killing for four weeks. That was a bit of a worry, but it was infinitely better than acquiring cerebral malaria, which can kill permanently.

Having learned from past experience what they might be, I avoided playing with the little items in the pretty packets. I wondered what men were doing when I saw them stop at a stall and pick up something on a string, until I realised that they were lighting their cigarettes from communal lighters.

It was now raining solidly. The blackest, inkiest cloud settled over the town and dropped a huge torrent of water. Relaxing on my veranda, watching the rain fall down where it couldn't get at me, I thought that this was definitely the way to enjoy a storm. Within minutes the side street was a flowing, muddy stream and the road in front of the guesthouse wasn't much better. A bevy of almost naked kids ran around playing soccer on the grass behind the houses and the ducks were having a ball.

At dinner time I decided that sloshing through the pouring rain in pitch-dark streets wasn't a good idea, so I ate downstairs in the café and watched another video with the staff – a most repulsively gung-ho African adventure that thrilled the others to bits.

I had discovered that I could travel from Kampot to Phnom Penh by the train which comes down one day, goes on to Sihanoukville, sleeps the night there and returns to Kampot and on to Phnom Penh the next day. I was told the train travels very slowly but slowly is not a problem for me. In fact it is something I have begun to covet.

Unlike Battembang, the locals didn't warn me off the train, and so, telling myself that they should know, I determined to give it a go. As I packed my bag, I wondered if my formerly lemon shirt was good enough to give to somebody rather than consign it to the bin. It had come back from another tryst with the laundry, this time having metamorphosed into a sort of mucky light brown with not quite all the Battembang dust and sunscreen stains removed. Having seen how our guide Sim had unashamedly worn a T-shirt with a great many holes in it, I didn't think anyone would turn up their nose at my shirt, so I gave it to one of the Mealy Chandra lads.

It rained heavily again in the night and I heard what I thought was someone chanting for hours in the rice fields behind the guesthouse. I later learned that it was a big toad.

In the morning I was waiting in the café for transport to the railway station when I received a nasty shock. Just when I had summoned the courage to ride the train, it had crashed! A bedraggled Mexican lad staggered in. He had just survived the train wreck. The train had been on its way from Sihanoukville when the heavy rain had caused a derailment. The Mexican said that he had been the only foreigner among the twenty or so passengers in the train's one carriage. The rest of the train had consisted of goods trucks. He said that the passenger carriage had two-person wooden seats and two guards totting AK-47s. Suddenly the train had lurched violently, swayed, and toppled over onto its side. The other passengers, who were mostly barefoot peasants, began jumping out of the windows on the opposite side. They thought that the train was being held up, as it had often been in the past by the Khmer Rouge guerrillas or bandits. The carriage and several goods wagons were tipped off the rails. The passengers were retrieved and transported to Kampot by bamboo train. Some were hurt, but no one was killed.

It would take weeks to fix the train line, so I had to resort to Plan B. The Mealy Chandra's obliging manager arranged for me to join a share taxi that was leaving for Phnom Penh the following morning. I told this charming boy that I wanted a driver who was really slow and careful. He swore that this driver was exactly that, extremely slow and careful. And, he said, 'He's very, very old.'

He looked about forty. His tiny car had the standard cracked windscreen and dashboard decorated with a scent bottle and a pagoda – the equivalent of a holy picture – for protection. He was a slight improvement on the young horror who had brought me to Kampot, but if he was slow and careful, fast and reckless is not something I ever wish to see.

The price I had negotiated had been five dollars for two seats. This gave me exclusive rights to the front seat which, despite its being a bucket seat, would normally have had two passengers occupying it. I really would have preferred the back seat, but four people were already compressed into that, three young English travellers and a Cambodian lady. They looked most uncomfortable, but told me that the taxi they had arrived in from Sihanoukville had carried eight people.

Off we roared, in pelting rain, on a road that was narrow, winding and slippery, but fairly good bitumen if you turned a blind eye to the potholes.

The countryside was green on green – rice paddies, banana and palm trees. Villages were frequent, and cows and pigs dotted the roadsides. The cows were always tethered, but not the pigs. They are intelligent enough to have road sense and remember where they live. There was much traffic – cars, vans, bicycles and motos – and we crossed plenty of bridges with the usual rattle of wooden boards underneath our wheels. We had several near misses when motos or vans almost scraped my side of the car. I oohed and ahhed and covered my eyes, putting the brakes on with both feet. I was jammed so close under the dashboard that I had visions of two broken legs. After a while I realised why the car felt strange. It was a right-hand drive vehicle. I was in the driver's seat! No wonder things kept scraping my side. The driver couldn't see properly.

It took three hours to reach Phnom Penh and it was a great relief to get there. Halfway into the journey it had stopped raining and now the sky was overcast and the weather humid. A few kilometres from the town we passed the Shooting Fields, an artillery range where soldiers earn extra cash by allowing tourists to play with lethal weapons for a fee. Twenty-five dollars will buy you the unalloyed joy of firing oodles of bullets from an AK-47. Twice that and you can go berserk with a machine gun, or blast a rocket launcher at a make-believe tank. For two hundred dollars they will provide a live cow for your pleasure.

Coming into the main part of Phnom Penh we drove along the longest avenue of heavily flowered frangipani trees that I have ever seen. We dropped off the Cambodian lady, then, helped by the other travellers, I persuaded our driver to take us to the Number Nine Guesthouse on Boeng Kak Lake, where previously I'd had lunch one day, and where we all planned to stay.

Number Nine is a very popular place and I couldn't get a room with a bathroom for the first night. The room I did get was at the rear and daggy. It cost three dollars, so that was not surprising. Only half of the ceiling was lined, the rest was just the green plastic of the roof. There was no latch on the door, the walls were rough wooden planks and so was the floor, large cracks allowed me a view of the opaque jade-green water of the lake underneath. No need to worry about a spill. Two large double beds filled the room and were the sum total of the furnishings. I had been hoping for a bed sheet for mozzie protection, but I was out of luck.

My room may have been definitely No Frills, but the taste of Khmer life was interesting. I had always thought these wooden houses on stilts in the water looked intriguing and had wanted to know what it would be like to stay in one. I suppose that, plagued by mosquitoes and with no mod cons, they are not so comfortable for people who have to live in them out of necessity.

The communal toilet facilities were extremely basic. I spent ages searching for the shower before I discovered that I had been in the room with it for quite some time. It was a pipe on the wall of the hole-in-the-floor toilet. The washbasin was on the outside wall, where teeth cleaning became a public exhibition. There was no running water outside. Filling the basin was a bucket and dipper job.

I had lunch in the pavilion over the water at the far end of the guesthouse. Looking across at the far side of the lake, I could see the buildings of the city and, past them, a line of shanties that stretched all the way around the water's edge.

After siesta I explored my surroundings. Both sides of the narrow, rutted lane were lined with tiny shops and cafés and off it ran a maze of dirt paths that all ended at the water. Some paths led to other guesthouses. There is no direct public access to the lake; you can only reach it via someone's property. I walked through a couple of guesthouses to check them out. This often necessitated negotiating my way through the mess of the laundry and kitchen to reach the business end. Then, surprisingly, I would come to the water and there would be a pleasant pavilion positioned over it.

Finding an internet overseas phone office, I made a call to my friend Min in Australia. It was her ninety-fifth birthday. Returning up the lane I had to step around a small flock of sheep that free-ranged there, fossicking for food in the gutters among the piles of rubbish. Hardly pure merinos, they were ugly, ungainly creatures with long legs and wool that hung down in untidy tatters and made them look like thoroughly seedy characters. One had a teeny baby over which she stood guard as it rested against a wall.

Back at Number Nine, waiting for my dinner, I read my guidebook. 'North of the lake is Phnom Penh's brothel district, best kept away from. Drunken Khmers shoot each other here,' the writer calmly stated. It was bad luck that I was already comfortably installed near to this nefarious location. I talked to a young skinny English girl who had been on the hippy trail for eight months. She looked like she could do with a good feed, but she had a sweet face and was terrifyingly sincere. The other guests here were also dreadfully young, but that was fair enough, it was that kind of place. The first bloke I sat down beside was rolling himself a joint from a tin and I could smell ganja everywhere, especially at night. It wafted into my room from the room next door through the cracks in the walls. At any time of the day I could find limp individuals lying about in hammocks, zonked out. Although marijuana is no longer officially legal in Cambodia, and the days when guesthouses placed bowls of it on the dining table are gone, it is still used in traditional cooking.

As the sky darkened, a girl set a lighted mosquito coil in a glass Fanta bottle, beside me on the board floor. The young folk played deafening music all day and half the night, but my earplugs helped.

The next day I lurked near the 'office', an open counter on one side of the café, waiting to bag the room that Oliver and Clare, the English couple with whom I had travelled up from Kampot, were vacating. It was the best in the house, on the far end of a single row of wooden rooms that marched on wooden stilts out into the water. It had, oh bliss, two windows, one on the side and one on the end that opened directly over the lake. A water plant with broad, brilliant green leaves grew thickly all around the lake's edges and was prevented from taking over the rooms only by woven rattan barriers.

Number Nine was entirely made of wood. The walkways of uneven boards alongside the rooms had a wooden rail on the water side to prevent falls into the drink. This rail was missing where the walkway ended at my door. And there was no light. One step too many in the dark and I would have had a baptism by total immersion. Baptism by muck, more likely. Although the water looked gorgeous and green, it was full of gunk. In an effort to remove the accumulated rubbish, every day the guesthouse staff scooped a large wire crab net on a pole through the water that surrounded their establishment. I hate to think what went into the lake. All the toilets from the rooms for a start.

When I climbed into bed in my room, I entered a green tent created by the bright green mosquito net that encapsulated it. I felt like a fish in an aquarium. My previous night's room had offered a peach coloured net and frill. Gazing out from that peach contraption, I had felt like a character from the *Arabian Nights*, or like a genie in a bottle.

Now I was glad of the family-sized tin of fly spray that I had bought in Kampot. I fumigated my room and my net each night. Battalions of mozzies, big enough to throw a saddle over, lurked hopefully outside my unscreened, glassless windows after dark. These assassins were only waiting for the dinner gong to announce that it was time to gallop in and attack me.

My new room had a bathroom, which after a day of deprivation I saw as a blessing; although it was primitive, it was sheer luxury compared to not having one at all. A marvel of simple engineering, the bathroom had a tiled floor and a very low loo that was flushed by dippering water from a conveniently placed bucket. Everything went into the lake. The drainage from the shower flowed down a hole in the corner towards which the floor sloped. There was no hand basin. I washed by taking a mandi, using the bucket and dipper method that I prefer when it's hot and the only available water is cold. My room had no equipment whatsoever apart from the bed, the mosquito net and the fan, which was fixed on the wall opposite the bed, but I loved it. I could lie in bed and watch the water and, buffeted by the wind, I really felt as though I was living on the lake.

As I strolled to breakfast after a wonderful sleep, the gentle morning sun lay on the orchids that hung in clay pots from the edges of the walkway roof. There were pure white orchids, white ones with purple hearts and many shades of mauve and purple. Two enormous snails inched their way to freedom from the morning's pile of sludge that had been fished from the lake with the crab pole net and now lay on the wooden walkway.

After brekkie I decided to head for the Russian market, Psar Tuoi Tom Pong, where you can buy a staggering variety of goodies including ganja, ready-rolled or in bulk. Outmanoeuvring the moto riders who lay in ambush at the front of Number Nine and who wanted twice the going rate, I found a rider who offered me the real price and off we bumped up the rough dirt track. Turning into a wider dirt lane that leads to the grand mosque further along the edge of the lake, we turned again and entered the traffic of Monivong Boulevard, one of Phnom Penh's main roads.

The Russian market (I could never discover why travellers

called it that) is not as big as the Central market and it had some touristy stuff, but some of it was interesting and well made compared to the ghastly rubbish considered suitable to foist onto tourists in other countries. It was, however, stiflingly hot in there. Tripping through the meat and fish section, side-stepping puddles of bloodstained water and dead fish in baskets or live ones in basins and buckets, I made it to the interior. Here two rows of women buzzed away on treadle sewing machines, sounding like a swarm of angry wasps. They would mend something while you waited, or make a new piece for you. I was running out of clothes and had brought a blouse and some material to have it copied. A time and a price were agreed upon, all by sign language, so I fervently hoped I wouldn't be in for a nasty surprise.

A woman selling post cards approached me. Her face was pathetically scarred and twisted, as though she had been dreadfully burned. I bought heaps. Then I loosened my rules and bought a couple of small souvenirs. There's no point having rules if you can't break them occasionally.

That day I was almost the victim of a robbery. I did something absolutely stupid and I should have known better. After having lunch at the Narine guesthouse, where I had stopped on the way back from the market, I paid at the office, which was practically on the street in a side alley. (Later I was told that this is a very bad area.) The sky was threatening rain, so I hailed a moto and jumped on, still with my small, soft leather purse in my hand. I slapped my hat on my head and, holding it on by its strings with the hand that still held the purse, we rode off. As usual, I had jammed my shopping bag between the rider and me and had its straps looped around my arm to stop anyone grabbing it.

We were sailing along the wide, busy Monivong Boulevard, when a moto came up close alongside us. Before I grasped what was happening – I simply could not believe it – the fellow on the pillion reached out, seized my purse and tried to snatch it away. But I was holding it firmly along with the strings of my hat and in a reflex action, tightened my grip. The would-be brigand pulled hard and nearly yanked me off the bike, but he did not get my purse. This all happened in a flash, but for a moment I looked at close range straight into the villain's eyes. What I saw there was chilling. Until then every Cambodian I had met had been smiling and amiable, but the owner of this grim, bad-looking face glared at me with total ill intent.

At the moment of contact I had given a shriek of fright and my moto driver became upset. Fortunately we didn't fall off and I was told that I was lucky. Many victims have been pulled off by the straps of their bags and been badly injured.

As we continued on to Number Nine, my driver kept turning around and asking, 'You okay, you okay?' He couldn't wait to dash off and tell the other drivers who hang around the guesthouses at the lake. I felt a complete fool and was angry with myself for being such a dill. I didn't realise how perturbed I was until I went to pay my rider and my hands were shaking so badly I could hardly count out his money. It was the evil purpose I had seen in the bandit's face that unnerved me. I was sure that, if he had been able, he would have stuck a knife in me to make me let go of that purse.

In the market I had bought a huge hand of bananas and they protruded from the top of my shopping bag. I think that this was why the man who assaulted me didn't want my bag. It looked to be full of fruit. Previously, when I'd had to walk nywhere in the dark at night, I had always clutched the strap of my handbag as tightly as possible and told myself that if someone took my bag they'd have to take me with it. Now the thought occurred to me that this time they very nearly did.

After this incident I became, even more than usual, an item of curiosity. My guesthouse family told everyone that I had foiled a robbery. I suppose I was targeted because a little old lady like me appeared less likely to resist than one of those big strapping wenches who heave backpacks around. Now they reckoned I was a tough old bird.

It finally rained in Phnom Penh, washing away some of the dust and dirt. It was not as hot beside the lake as in the city centre, but I had felt the heat during my first siesta, and endured two solid hours of sweating, as though I was in a sauna, before I discovered that the fan switch was outside my door on the wall of the walkway. The wind and the rain increased and, looking out of the window, I suddenly had the feeling that my room was moving as though it was a boat. Then I realised that the wind on the water of the lake had set the waterweed in motion and it was moving, not me.

At dinner I had the entire pavilion to myself. The wimps had deserted it when the rain had started to blow in. I thought it was exciting. The wind and the water rocked the pavilion and flashes of vivid lightning streaked across the grey dusk sky to shoot into the green weed.

In my room the rain began pouring in my windows, which could only be closed by the wooden louvred shutters. Water still flooded in after I had pulled them across, but I was not fussed – the water rolled down the floor, ran through the cracks between the boards and disappeared into the lake. Rain came in the door too, but it went out again the same way. But the drumming and swishing grew louder and louder, and I drew the line when water started flying in and wetting my bed. That's when I got up and stuffed my towel in the crack between the window shutters. Being in the end room and having the luxury of an extra window that faced the lake came at a price. Once the storm had blown in, it settled down to a steady rain that went on for hours. At six in the morning I pushed open my shutters. The rain had cleared, the sky was bright blue and early light was soft on the buildings of the far shore. A fisherman paddled his canoe on the grey-green water under my window. He was following the edge of the weed and collecting something from among it. His boat was tiny and narrow and he sat, seemingly precariously, only inches off the water on one end. Further out another man in a canoe carefully manoeuvred a net, slowly hauling it in, hand over hand, to pile alongside him in the canoe. The booty in the net looked slim pickings. A loud honking came from the direction of the railway station; as the train left, the noise moved further away until it disappeared.

At Number Nine I lived among the extended families of the owners and workers. As I ate my breakfast, a naked baby crawled, teetered and fell about among the tables, a toddler rode a very ritzy tricycle up and down with fine disregard for passing ankles, and Grandma, minus teeth and hair but otherwise still intact and gracefully erect, walked barefoot past me dressed in a sarong. The boys of the family had started calling me Mummy. I had thought it nice when I was called Sister, as they call each other brother and sister – but Mummy? I supposed it was better than Daddy and after all I was at least twice the age of everyone there.

I asked the staff how I could get to the suburb in outer Phnom Penh where Australian Geraldine Cox and her sixty-five orphans live. They organised a tuk tuk to take me there, but firstly the tuk tuk driver and I had to find a street phone so that someone at Geraldine's could give him directions in Khmer.

It had taken me a while to realise that the tiny cubes of dark brown glass I saw in the street were public phones. They had lots of large white numbers pasted on them, and I had thought that they traded lottery tickets or some such commodity. A woman attendant sat on a chair beside the booth and sold you time on her mobile phone at the rate of twenty-five cents a minute for a local call; the same rate as a call to Australia from the phone office.

Today, I didn't have enough riels, so I had to borrow the money from my tuk tuk driver. Once we'd been given instructions it still took us about forty minutes to find Geraldine

Cox's house. After being misdirected several times by well-meaning people whom the driver asked for help, we finally ended up at a big gate on which I banged for admission. Then, as soon as I was inside, sixty-five delightful children surrounded me.

They all live in a big two-storey house with a large basement, in which one of the women helpers lay recovering from typhoid – I was glad then of my inoculations. The gorgeous children were thrilled to have a visitor – they came up, made a sompiah, took my hand and beamed at me. Then they sat me on a chair, gave me a glass of water and six of them danced for me.

The dancers had coconut shells which they clapped together, while behind them one boy beat on an instrument that looked like a gamelan and another thumped a drum. These tiny children, no more than five or six years old, remembered long and intricate routines that, as a line dancer, I am here to tell you I could no more have remembered than fly. They not only moved their feet, but also their heads, while their little hands made graceful gestures.

We ate lunch outside at long communal tables under a pergola. Nothing was fancy. Washing hung all around and the washing up was done in a series of bowls on the ground. Everyone helped. The kids sleep in rows of hammocks. Everything was clean and the children looked happy.

I liked Geraldine Cox. And I was really glad that I had made the effort to find her. When I told her that I was staying at Guesthouse Number Nine. She said, 'Oh, that's where all the druggies and hippies hang out.'

'Yeah, baby. Right on,' I replied.

Geraldine is doing a phenomenal job. Her operation is not one of those high profile charity businesses where much of the money goes into administration. The children get it all. They don't leave Geraldine until they are eighteen and have a job. I really liked the fact that she is not destroying their culture and heritage, or changing them into little Westerners. They have daily Buddhist religious instruction, but they also learn English and everyone over seven is taught computer skills.

I patted the old mongrel dog that one of the kids brought home as a puppy. Geraldine told me that she had said, 'We don't need a dog,' but was undone when the boy came back with: 'He's an orphan, you have to have him. I found him all alone.'

I asked how she acquires the children. Does she just pick them up in the street?

'No way,' she said. Headmen of villages usually approach her when, for example, a man is killed by a land mine and the wife can't cope and runs off.

Geraldine has been made a Cambodian citizen by the king, who must like children – he has sixty odd of his own. We parted friends with a hug and I tuk-tuked back to Number Nine. Geraldine's story can be found in her book, My Khmer Heart.

I went to the Russian market again to pick up my new blouse. On the way I asked the moto driver to take me to the bank. Instead, he took me to a moneychanger convenient to the road, who did the transaction very adroitly. This rider wore a helmet, the first I had seen in Cambodia. It seemed to give him added courage, though it did nothing to increase mine. I had seen riders in races drag their legs on the ground as they cornered and this fellow was trying to do that. I didn't like it a lot. I expected any minute to feel my leg scraping the road.

Suddenly Action Man turned into Evil Knievel. We bounced up a curb, shot across a petrol station and went flying off the gutter at the other side landing with a bump, but fortunately right side up. By this time I had the driver in a half Nelson. As we landed on our wheels again, we passed a little red car so closely I brushed it with my leg. It was one of those tiny cars that look as though it has been bought by someone with only enough money to pay for the front part.

I had a lovely time in the market, met some agreeable stall-holders and made it there and back safely with a whole lot of loot. For someone who wasn't ever buying souvenirs again I did pretty well. And I'd had to invest in a new handbag. I might have survived the trip so far, but my handbag hadn't. I finally twigged that the bits of black skin that I kept finding stuck to my damp sweaty arms were from the gradual disintegration of my indispensable handbag, out of which I could survive for at least a fortnight, as well as perform the odd bit of surgery. It had been brand new when I had started out on this trip, but it had had a rough time and now was fit for the bin.

Later, resting in my room, I watched the last rays of the sun setting across the lake and streaming in through my open window. A gentle breeze combined with the fan to keep me beautifully cool, as well as dry my blouse that swung to and fro on the string that held up my green mosquito net. My bed at home was about as big as the one in this room, but I don't take piles of my possessions to bed with me there. You need to tuck the mosquito net in all around the bed once you get in to it and this makes it a safe place to keep your knitting, book, glasses and what not.

I would like to have visited Skuon, a village whose claim to fame is that it is known as Spiderville after a peculiar culinary taste the locals have acquired. Not that I have any desire for an arachnoid snack, but I would like to have seen someone else indulge in this dubious treat. The inhabitants of Skuon apparently developed this gastronomic habit during the famine years of the Khmer Rouge. But I had to forgo the visit. My visa to re-enter Vietnam was about to expire and I had to leave. The staff at Number Nine arranged a ticket on the boat that travels down the river from Phnom Penh to Vietnam, via Chou Doc, for me.

The day I had chosen to leave was a Saturday and for the first time I did not hear trains honking in the morning. Utter stillness lay on the silver waters of the lake with their dark green islands of weed, as the rising sun lit the buildings across the way with a lovely pinkish glow. Then all the lake turned rosy. I heard the gentle flip of water off a paddle and a man floated by in his canoe. Another drifted with the movement of the water. Everything seemed to be in slow motion. That's part of the charm of Cambodia.

My boat ticket included transport to the riverside, but it was not due to collect me until two, so I took off to photograph the elephant that always stood outside Wat Phnom. There I met a Khmer man and the three enchanting children he had brought to see the elephant. I paid one dollar fifty to buy the beast some bananas, which was the asking price for taking a photo. The elephant scoffed down my exorbitantly priced bananas whole, skins and all, in one go. I could have climbed up into his howdah, but it looked extremely rickety and I was feeling lazy, so I went for a walk instead.

I thought I knew a short cut from Wat Phnom to the post office and soon, turning a corner and expecting a further hike, I was surprised to find myself right beside it. On the way back to Number Nine I passed a man on a moto who carried rows of chooks strung along both sides of his machine. I had seen this sight before and had assumed that the birds were dead, but this time I had a close look and saw one fowl trying to peck the ground. They were alive! Once before I had seen a dainty girl sitting side-saddle on a pillion carrying what I thought at first was a pile of feather dusters, until I saw that it was an enormous fowl hanging down over her knees. Sometimes I saw motorbikes that were so completely covered in live ducks and hens that they looked like feathered monsters.

I sat in the pavilion waiting for the minibus that was to take me to the boat. It was the hottest day I had known at the lake, but black clouds were marshalling across the water. As I paid my bill I decided that adding up your own account at the end of your stay really didn't work in favour of the establishment. I was quite sure that the sum I arrived at wasn't enough and, even though I told him this, the manager only laughed and insisted it was okay. I must have eaten a lot more food than I had been charged for – thirty-eight dollars for four nights stay and four days worth of food seemed ridiculous.

The minibus was busy, so a couple of English girls and I were taken to the river in the guesthouse owner's car. Considering the simple way in which the family lived, they had a most up-market car. It was the latest Toyota Camry and was covered in gadgets and accessories including, hanging off the back of the driver's seat in a ritzy holster, a business-like magnum .38 pistol. The boy drove like a loony to the riverboat dock where an immigration officer, housed in a small cubicle, took our passports from us. I was ashamed of the state of mine. The poor thing had begun these travels brand new, but now it had a permanent bend from being stuffed in its holder, hung from a string around my neck, and shoved into the elastic waist of my pants. Eight foreigners, including three young Vikings – actually they were Danes who filled two seats each – were taking this boat down the Mekong to Vietnam, along with some Cambodians including a mother, father and little girl, all of whom wore utterly gruesome hats. At the pre-destined time we were trundled down the gangway, led by the immigration official carrying my bag. Having seen us safely on our way, he shook hands and went back to his cubicle.

We voyagers clambered down into a speedboat that had about twenty seats arranged in double rows facing the front. The fore and aft hatches were kept open, which made it very breezy, but this was a relief after the heat of the town. We proceeded down the river, collecting a few spots of rain on the way.

Viewed from the water Phnom Penh's riverside is very attractive. We cruised past the royal palace and other grand buildings along the cornice and before long we were in the country. Then, except for the green river bank and the odd hovel of a village, I didn't see much for a long time. It was only when we approached the border that villages became more frequent. We travelled on the River Bassac, which joins the Mekong at Phnom Penh, and for most of the way we followed close to one or the other riverbank. Banana trees, bamboo and coconut palms raised their heads above the low greenery growing along the water's edge framing the skyline. Occasionally the red-and-yellow-spired roof of a small, open-sided pagoda appeared among the dense green jungle. The few dwellings near the pagodas were shanties of grey wood and bamboo that looked falling-down poor. I saw only one community that was big enough to call a town.

The river traffic was light until we drew near to the border. We arrived at the Cambodian immigration post to find the most impeccably groomed, tree-shaded, flower-bedecked place imaginable. We were helped off the boat and onto a wee landing. Walking up an immaculately swept path, we were seated at a long table with a dark blue tablecloth. Everyone was charming. A smiling official took our passports away and returned them to us in half an hour. It was a downright refined process. We had already been given the necessary forms to fill out on the boat, which had proved no mean feat in a craft that was bobbing madly up and down. I doubt that mine was legible.

Loaded back on the boat, in a few more minutes we were at the Vietnamese border post. This was pretty run-down compared to the Cambodian one. It was housed in three small stone offices on the edge of the riverbank around which a few cows wandered. In the first office, a polite young man gave me a quarantine form to fill out. A handwritten chart on the wall listed numerous vaccinations and their cost. You were obliged to have all of these punched into you if you couldn't prove that your body already contained them. Fortunately I was able to produce my yellow vaccination book, which confirmed my disease-free state, but I had to pay a fee for being certified as such. It cost two thousand dong, twenty-three cents, for which price I received a meticulously handwritten receipt.

I sat on the riverbank and talked to one of the young Vikings for half an hour while we waited for the driver of the boat, who was taking care of the immigration rites for us. No customs officers fossicked through our bags, which was a nice change.

We travelled on. Now the river traffic was dense. The air was thick with smoke, possibly from burning rice stubble in the Vietnamese paddies. A further hour onwards and we drew near Chou Doc.

9 Chou Doc – No Pain, No Gain

As we approached Chou Doc, the riverbank became lined with ever more shanties – better-class, more substantial ones, now that we were in Vietnam. Our craft navigated past a tatty landing barge busy with passengers and vehicles, pulled into the bank and put the Cambodians ashore.

Now only the other foreigners and I were left aboard as we inched back out into the main stream of the river to move past rows of fish farms. At first glance these appeared to be normal wooden houses that had lost their way and ended up out in the middle of the river, but closer scrutiny revealed that they were floating on metal drums and permanently anchored. The fish were farmed in cages under and around them.

At six o'clock we docked at a small landing that I was told was Chou Doc. There were no steps and it was a steep leg-up to the top of the bank, but a kind young girl leaned down and hauled me ashore. A man offered me a ride in his cyclo and I negotiated a price to the hotel I had selected from the guide-book. The cyclo was not the usual specimen of that breed. More of a freight wagon, it had no overhead covering and was entirely constructed from bright, flashing aluminium slats – even the seat was just a bent piece of slat. It was not in the least bit comfortable, but it surely shone like silver.

This contraption delivered me to the hotel, where a young man gave me a room and informed me of the sad news that the hydrofoil boat, on which I had planned to proceed to Saigon, had been made redundant.

'Maybe another boat, but slow one,' he said, and phoned the number for it. But there was no room for me on the slow boat, so the hotel person sold me a ticket for a bus that left Chou Doc for Saigon – Ho Chi Minh City – at half past eight the next morning.

The Thuan Loi Hotel perches right on the edge of the riverbank and has a close-up view of the busy river life all around it, especially from the downstairs café which is in a veranda that sits on stilts in the water. As it was dinnertime, the café was my first stop. I took a seat on the edge of the veranda, where the passing boats were almost level with me as I ate. The café possessed a board floor and was decked out with – what else? – blue plastic chairs. The cook moved around igniting incense coils against the million or so mozzies that joined my welcoming committee.

As I watched, a house went by, pulled by a tug. Other houseboats, moored to the riverside by ropes, bobbed up and down around me on the barrels they used as floats. They had plants, dogs and kids a-plenty on board, and outhouses tacked onto their rear-ends over the water. A woman was doing the washing on a nearby houseboat, squatting on the narrow rim of the deck and dousing the clothes in a bucket of water drawn from the river. The riverfront house next door to the hotel was so close I could have reached out and touched the owner as he tended the orchids that hung in pots from his blue balcony.

I was again surprised by the low standards of the authors of my guidebook. They had said that this hotel had pleasant sitting areas on its balconies. These blokes must be very easily pleased. On investigation this cosy haven proved to be half a metre wide, with two concrete stools.

I thought I had mastered the art of using the diabolical wall showers common to this part of the world. First you punched in the big button, then you pushed in another underneath it, then you turned the knob to the required temperature, hot, cold, or indifferent, and lastly, you turned on the volume regulator. I did all this, then in reverse, but I still wasn't rewarded with hot water. Then I noticed a sign on the wall and, putting on my glasses, read the English translation. It said, 'If you wanting hot water stand in the bucket'.

It wasn't a terribly big bucket and I really couldn't see what standing in the bucket was going to do. But I eventually worked out that it didn't mean that you should stand in the bucket, you stood the shower head in the bucket and, for some obscure reason, this conjured up hot water.

My room also came with a communal comb, a large pink one. Not quite the same as Cambodian communal combs, this one didn't have a handle, but it was a real bug-rake.

A line of pictures with Vietnamese captions decorated the wall. Even an ignoramus like I, who couldn't read them, understood that the pictures were telling me what I shouldn't bring into the room. After a careful study of the artwork I deduced that it was lucky I had left my AK-47, all my bombs and particularly my nuclear explosive devices outside, as the management would not have let me in with them.

My passport, which had been taken into protective custody by the local constabulary the previous night, was released in the morning. I was back in a police state. Some hotels and guesthouses in Cambodia did not even ask you to register and when they did, they weren't interested in seeing your passport. If you wrote down its number, they took your word for it.

The hotel manager banged on my door and dragged me from my room at twenty past eight. I thought that the bus must be at the door, but I was wrong. The bus did not make house calls. My bag was thrown onto one motorbike, I was hauled onto another and off we went to search for it.

Eventually we found its lair – a hole in the wall, alleged to be a bus station, where numerous folk squatted on pygmy plastic stools. (I won't tell you what colour.) I joined the throng and after about half an hour the bus appeared. Watching the passing parade, I realised that I was now back in coolie hat country instead of the karma scarves worn in Cambodia.

An elderly gentleman who spoke English approached me and told me proudly that he, too, was an Australian. He was one of the boat people who had escaped from Vietnam following the fall of Saigon many years ago and had settled in Melbourne. Mr Tran, deciding that I was in need of a protector, immediately took full responsibility for my care and feeding. I was the only foreigner on the bus and no one else spoke English, so I was grateful for his help. It can be difficult to know when a possible loo is reached – I usually wait until I see the ladies stampeding off in one general direction and follow them.

Deciding that my bag needed a seat to itself, I indicated to the conductor that I wanted to buy the empty seat beside me, and, with my friend interpreting for me, I did so. It cost three dollars fifty as opposed to the five dollars I had paid at the hotel, but was worth it not to have someone crammed on top of me, as this turned out to be a long ride.

Kids ride free, but they have to sit on your lap. I felt sorry for the people travelling with big children. One man nearby was struggling to hold his little girl as well as a large bag on his lap, so I let him put his bag on top of mine while she sat on his lap all the way to Saigon. Well-behaved and a real little doll, this two-year-old was dressed to the nines in a frilly pink organza dress that had rose buds made of ribbon sewn all over it. I had been surprised at the number of Cambodian and Vietnamese men I had seen taking care of children and babies. I had imagined that they would be far too macho.

Driving slowly through the centre of Chou Doc, which is quite a large town, we were shortly in suburbs that consisted of rows of tiny, single-storey wooden houses, many of which were mere hovels that stood with their feet in water. There was water everywhere. The wide River Bassac flowed alongside us on one side, the canal in which the houses stood was on the other, and there were also many ponds on which ducks dabbled and fish jumped. On the outskirts of Chou Doc the bus was stopped at a police inspection point and an officer climbed aboard and looked in all the luggage racks and under the seats. As the only foreigner I expected to be interrogated, but I was ignored. I think officialdom was only interested in the smuggling activities of the locals, which I believe are many and varied.

Evidence of the recent harvest was all around. Drying rice lay on black shadecloth like carpets of gold between the houses, the ponds and the road, sometimes only inches from our wheels. I saw four fat pigeons having a wonderful time in one lot. They must have thought that they had landed in pigeon heaven.

The Mekong delta is heavily populated and the land was pretty much built up all the way to Saigon, except for one area where huge expanses of paddy grew in big paddocks, rather than the usual diminutive plots. Further on sweet corn, maize, bamboo and vegetables were under cultivation. In every rice paddy the tombs of the family's ancestors stood keeping watch. I didn't see many rice field tombs in Cambodia; perhaps they had all been destroyed. But once, beside an ordinary wooden plank house, I had seen a magnificent, many-coloured tomb and the thought had occurred to me that the dead ancestor had a much better house than his living rellies. In front of the house ponds that lined the road in one village, hundreds of crabs had been laid on the ground to dry, while hundreds more were arranged in neat rows on long wooden trestles.

The bus developed wheel problems and we stopped at a mechanic's shop by the side of the road. This enterprise consisted of two poles holding a piece of blue plastic tarpaulin over an enormous assortment of objects stacked high on rough board shelves. There was no way this emporium could have been locked at night, so someone must have slept in the humpy at the rear to protect it.

The seat in front of me in the bus held a little girl of about three, her mother and grandmother. Grandma was a frail, diminutive person and all I could see of her from behind were her hands. I was fascinated to see that she was teaching the child the intricate finger movements of the Aspara dance. She would twirl her hands up and around and the small child would imitate the movements. And quite well too.

The journey to Saigon took more than seven hours. After the halfway point a decent house began to appear now and then, but they were still only single-storey. Later came multi-storeyed dwellings, and then towns. We crossed the Bassac on a ferry at Cantho, where the channel was hugely wide, and later, in the heart of the delta, crossed countless bridges over countless sheets of water, all of which were teeming with boats, big and small.

I had been waiting for the lunch break, but we didn't stop anywhere for a meal. This surprised me as I had become accustomed to travellers in Asia halting frequently to feed. Whenever the bus had stopped for petrol, wheel fixing, or other necessities, sellers had boarded with goodies in baskets on their heads. I resisted these enticements to disaster – the food was unwrapped and the fruit peeled – for as long as I could. Then a woman came up the aisle bearing a great, lidded aluminium pot on her head. It contained steamed dumplings kept hot with live coals. I bought one. The outer casing tasted the same as the white paper it was wrapped in. I know this because it was also the same colour as the paper and I ate a mouthful of that by mistake. The inside of the dumpling, although of indeterminate origin, was tasty enough and it kept me from starvation.

It was evening by the time we reached Saigon, where the bus did a taxi run all over town dropping people off. I was the last to leave as I didn't know where the bus was going to end up and I certainly didn't know where I was. I showed a moto rider the card my former hotel had given me and when I rocked up in front of it, the manager rushed into the street to help me dismount. Actually, it was more like falling off. It had taken me this long, almost at the end of my journey, to discover why I always stumbled off motos in an untidy heap. The riders tip the bike sideways to help you alight. You are supposed to already have your feet on the ground by then, but because I am a bit slow what it does to me is throw me onto the road.

The hotel manager gave me the room I'd had before, but I bargained him down a little for the use of a fan instead of the air conditioner. Then I went out to get my film developed and acquire some food. I returned to the café in which I had eaten on my last night in Saigon, the new place where I had been their first customer. The staff, who had been so thrilled to snare me that night, remembered me, and how could they forget? I was probably wearing the same loud shirt. The little waitress put her arm around me and gave me tiny pats and hugs. The Vietnamese are lovely people, but they seem like a bunch of sourpusses after the Cambodians, who are absolutely superb. I was glad to see that the café now had a good-sized mob of Westerners in there eating up big.

I took my trousers, which were on their last legs, to the tailor in the shop next door to the hotel and asked him to copy, and then jettison, them. Right or wrong he wanted to repair them. 'No way throw out!' he said, 'I mend.'

It took a lot of argument to convince him that I'd had them for more than twelve years and they had well and truly earned their final rest. I never throw out my clothes until they are beyond help.

Reluctantly the tailor agreed, but he still thought it was a terrible waste. I redeemed myself by telling him that he could have them afterwards and they are probably right now swanning around Saigon reincarnated. Born-again pants.

My last morning arrived. I was due to fly home late that afternoon. I filled in the time by having a happy rummage around the Ben Than market. You can buy great clothes cheaply in Saigon's shops and markets, but most of the souvenirs are truly repulsive. Garish and glaring, they are a legacy of US army tastes. But I liked the bottles of snake wine. I wouldn't be brave enough to drink it, but the pickled cobras glaring evilly out from the pretty bottles were, to say the least, attention-grabbing. As a lasting reminder of this pleasant journey in Indochina, I bought three of the non-removable bracelets the local women wear. The process of acquiring them, which takes two people – one pulling and one pushing – is rather like the bone-scrunching practice of Chinese foot binding. 'Only a little pain,' the vendor said as they were screwed on.

Now in departure mode, I packed my snake wine, caught a taxi to the airport and was on my way home.

Also by Wakefield Press

BEHIND THE VEIL
An Australian nurse in Saudi Arabia
Lydia Laube

Lydia Laube worked as a nurse in a society that does not allow women to drive, vote or speak to a man alone.

Wearing head to toe coverings in stifling heat, and battling administrative apathy, Lydia Laube kept her sanity and got her passport back.

Behind the Veil is the hilarious account of an Australian woman's battle against the odds. It will keep you entertained for hours.

ISBN 978 1 86254 267 9

THE LONG WAY HOME
Lydia Laube

Lydia Laube returns to Saudi Arabia, collects her pay, then decides to take the long way home via dangerous turf in Egypt, Sudan, Kenya and India.

Our Good Little Woman is as eccentric and entertaining as ever ... blithely she trots along, sunshade held aloft, while behind her ships sink, hotels explode, and wars erupt.

ISBN 978 1 86254 325 6

For more information visit www.wakefieldpress.com.au

Also by Wakefield Press

SLOW BOAT TO MONGOLIA
Lydia Laube

Who else but Lydia Laube would climb the Great Wall of China waving a pink parasol while riding a donkey? In *Slow Boat to Mongolia* Lydia tells of her travels by ship, train and bone-shaking bus through Indonesia and China on her way to fabled Outer Mongolia.

Lydia learns to use chopsticks with aplomb and ploughs her way through crowds to visit places few westerners have seen. She reaches Outer Mongolia, where she stays in a *ger* in the snow and rides a horse through waist-high silvery grass.

ISBN 978 1 86254 418 5

BOUND FOR VIETNAM
Lydia Laube

Lydia Laube never takes no for an answer. In *Bound for Vietnam*, against all protests, she finds ways to venture through rarely travelled parts of China, overcoming language barriers and standing her ground in crowded buses, boats and trains. She makes a meal of a snake and submits to the ministrations of the Dental Department of your worst nightmare.

Leaving China by pedal-power, Lydia enters Vietnam by motorbike and discovers a beautiful and resilient country.

Sit tight as you ride with our brave lone traveller. Her adventures will amaze and impress you.

ISBN 978 1 86254 462 8

For more information visit www.wakefieldpress.com.au